Stalking the Wild Dragonfly

Stories of Experiences in Nature

Vishnu Temple Press
Flagstaff, Arizona

Vishnu Temple Press
P. O. Box 30821
Flagstaff, Arizona 86003
(928) 556 0742
www.vishnutemplepress.com

Cover design by Sandra Kim Muleady.
Cover art from an original painting by ValJesse O'Feeney.
Interior art courtesy of ValJesse O'Feeney.

Stalking the Wild Dragonfly

Stories of Experiences in Nature
by
Nancy Rivest Green

DEDICATION

To all the marvelous wild animals who have allowed me to
glimpse fleeting segments of their fascinating lives,

and to Keith, who has shared
so many of these touching experiences with me.

This book is dedicated to Annette Schober,
an eloquent author who left this Earth much too soon.
She had a love and reverence for nature
that matches my own.

AUTHOR'S NOTE

Responsibility for any errors or misinterpretation of collected research data totally belongs to the author.

It is interesting to note that the more one researches, the more disparate the facts. It's obvious that the observation of animals becomes more subjective over time. It's hard to stay separate from animals once entering their world.

This is a work of creative non-fiction.

Just this morning, I encountered a herd of thirteen deer and a soaring hawk on my walk in the forest. I am a better person because of it.

Nancy Rivest Green
Earth Day
April, 2016
As I watch the forest through my library window coming back to life in springtime

Table of Contents

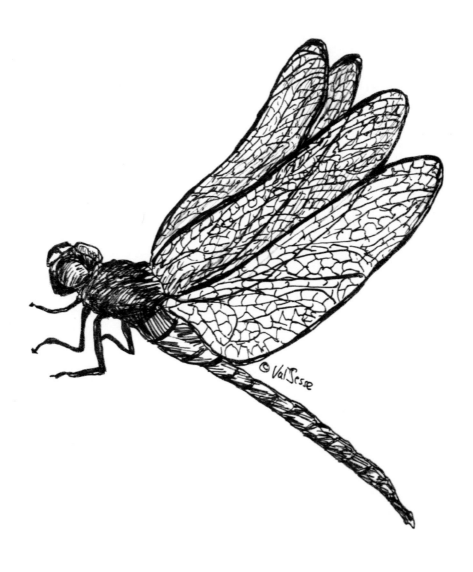

I
Dragonfly

We stopped to scout Hance Rapid. Most people hiked up the side of the cliff to view the rapid, the biggest they had seen so far on the upper portion of the Colorado River through the Grand Canyon. I stayed near the river.

A dragonfly drifts into view. Stopping six inches from my nose, it grabs a piece of waving grass with its tiny feet. I am astonished to be so close to a tethered dragonfly. It is a brilliant golden/burnt-orange, fluttering wings a golden flicker, reminiscent of medieval Spanish filigree. Clinging to the swaying grass, its shoulders work rhythmically, slender body moving as counterbalance to the biplane wings. The copper-colored head swivels between the stalk of grass in front of it, and me standing to the side of it. Its eyes beneath boxy eyelids check me out. This insect is sentient—something I have never considered about this life form. The spell breaks as it takes advantage of a gusty breeze to release from its tether and sail up river, fluttering wings tiny against the massive canyon cliffs. What a gift to share that moment with a dragonfly.

Since then, I have been thrilled time and again by the sight of dragonflies riding wave currents of air. Deep violet, pink, indigo blue, yellow, fiery red, emerald green, and copper wings shimmer in the summer sun as they dart past. Their favorite haunt is around water, but I have seen them deep in the forest away from any water source. Seeking the sun and wind for their mating ritual, they fly together in insect intercourse, all the more beautiful with two slender bodies and eight wings.

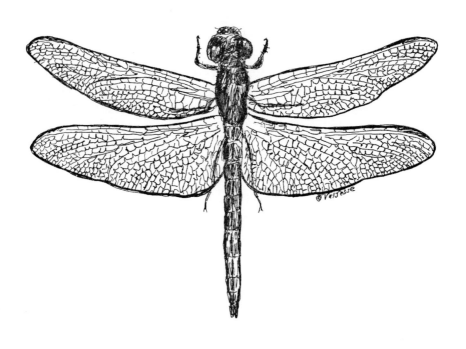

Dragonflies have withstood the test of time. Fossils have been found of dragonfly-like insects dating back 325 million years. 125 million years later, dragonflies like the ones we see today flew over the backs of swamp-dwelling dinosaurs. These ancient ones had a 30-inch wingspan, similar to a common tern, with a 16-inch body.

Today's largest is the Hawaiian dragonfly, with a 7-inch wingspan and 5-inch body, while today's smallest is ¾ of an inch. The hind wings are broader than the front wings, with all four wings having the ability to move independently.

Dragonflies have long been associated with water. Sometimes they lay their few dozen eggs scattered in wet mud or on floating vegetation in the water. Canyon streams deep in deserts have dragonflies skimming over standing water, and perching along the edges of moving water. After a muddy beginning, an adult bursts forth from the water, shedding its final skin in its long series of moltings. When the air temperature is 65-70°, they take to the air.

Dragonfly annual cycles of life make them a source of spiritual contemplation for Native Americans. Petroglyphs of dragonflies from the Mogollon Mimbres show the insect as a guide of the soul to the other side. Hopi associate the dragonflies with life-giving springs, Navajo with pools of water. The Zuni believe dragonflies are the messengers between humans and the gods. Dragonflies are seen as symbols of regeneration, transformation, birth, and death because of their magical emergence from water.

II
Pronghorn

The crew released the lines and we floated into the sky. A hint of golden horizon off to the east brightened the higher we rose. We were just south of Sonoita, Arizona, a land of high plateaus surrounded by desert mountains—the Santa Ritas, Huachucas, and Whetstones. As dawn light beamed out over the horizon, our view of the rolling hills and lush grasslands of Southern Arizona expanded.

The pilot occasionally touched a lever which gave a short, noisy blast on the burner, controlling our elevation. In between these dragon-like breaths, the only sound was air rushing by our ears.

Suddenly our ride was interrupted by a rhythmic pounding from the earth below. The four of us in the hot air balloon swiveled in every direction, wondering what could be making that powerful, insistent sound. We were too remote for anything man-made. It had to be a sound of nature.

From over a ridgeline they galloped, a herd of pronghorn. Brown bodies marked by striking swaths of white on the belly and neck, black smudge by the nose, and short double horns with a slight curve to the long shaft. They ran clumped together, coming toward the long shadow of the balloon. Without breaking stride, the twenty or so antelope glanced upwards at us, then increased their pace. From this height, their beauty and elegance could only be seen in broad strokes. I have seen them up close; their eyes are larger than an elephant's. The orbit of their vision allows for swiveling sideways or up and down, seeing present dangers as well as remembering past conflicts with huge, now extinct birds of prey. Perhaps this herd had that ancient memory, probably wondering if we were some sort of round condor.

I sensed the primal force of the herd with their rumps flashing white, legs pumping, puffs of dirt rising into the sun-streaked air from their frantic hooves. Their anxiety was fueled by this unknown threat. They were used to soaring hawks and golden eagles, and in the last millennia, the 9-foot wingspan of a condor. But what was this raindrop-shaped beast, with the occasional noisy, fiery breath? They could not know, but they could run, so they ran–up and over hills, through the lush grassland, until they pounded away from us and were gone, footfalls fading in the dawn. Seeing them from the air provided a new perspective of these engaging creatures.

All my years of living at Grand Canyon and driving back and forth to Flagstaff I saw them, sometimes just a glimpse, sometimes a full-on view of them lying down, sometimes running, other times just standing around catching up on pronghorn gossip. They would cluster in the open areas of prairie, in between stands of junipers. Once, I watched an exuberant youngster cut figure eights in between the more staid elders.

I have never seen a pronghorn killed by a car. Unlike the deer or elk, they are unable to jump the roadside fences. Once, in Parks, two pronghorn proved this. They ran across the road at full speed not far ahead of my car. Knowing the fence was there, they braked, then slid

to the ground with their legs thrown out in the shape of an X, and wriggled under the fence. Smart creatures.

Pronghorn genetic history goes back more than 10,000 years and coincides with the appearance of humans into North America. While the woolly mammoths, giant ground sloths, saber-tooth tigers, and dire wolves became extinct, the stalwart pronghorn made it to the present day.

Preferring the short grass prairies from east of the Rockies to Baja California, they adapted to various climates all along the way. Here the pronghorn's incredible speed is unhampered.

Prehistorically, bands of Native Americans noted the pronghorn's inability to clear high obstacles, and hunted communally to drive herds into high corrals made of sagebrush and juniper limbs, forcing the pronghorns to run in circles until the point of exhaustion. The Spanish introduction of horses made catching pronghorns much easier.

Lewis and Clark noted the abundance of pronghorns, and made a contribution to science by providing the first specimen. By the 1900s, a mere one hundred years later, pronghorns were on the brink of extinction. But last century's conservation efforts returned the pronghorn to an abundant level.

Their eyes have a dark pigment to help with the summer sun and the snows of winter. Their huge eyes help them inspect abnormalities in their environment, discern if there is danger, and flee only when necessary. They can make this decision from half a mile away, saving crucial energy from bolting needlessly. But if they need to get away, they can do so at 50 mph, moving air through their windpipe four and a half times faster than a human. With a heart twice as big as a sheep, and a built-in brain cooling system, this creature is born to run.

When seen straight on, the male antlers form a heart-shape. With their striped neck, white belly, brown sides and inquisitive stare, they are certainly the most strikingly beautiful hoofed creature in North America.

© Val Jesse

III
Elk

Late August an elk scratches his antlers violently on a young tree, rubbing away the velvet and sharpening his weapons. Next comes a sound that never fails to thrill, the high-pitched squealing of a bull elk in rut, looking for love. Sometimes the long bugling ends in a guttural grunt. The elk throws his huge head back over his shoulders, enormous antlers almost touching his back, nose extending to the sky. And on a cold day, a marvelous puff of steamy breath emerges from his open mouth.

But on a summer's day, it's the mama and babies who do the communicating. Once, Keetna and I were deep in the woods on the South Rim when we heard a thrashing in the forest off to the west. In front of us burst two spotted baby elk squealing louder than a two year old in full tantrum mode. Mama, with a slightly lower squeal, also appeared in front of us. By now, I had my excited dog back on her leash and sitting next to me. We waited quietly as Mama and babies reunited. The babies were trembling with fright from the perceived threat of my goofy black Lab, but Mama saw that all was well. After a glance at us, she turned tail, trotting to the east. The now thoroughly chastised and obedient babies stayed very close to her.

One blistering hot day, Keetna and I came upon an enormous bull elk resting in the shade. My black Lab, not the brightest crayon in the box of life, began circling around his bulk, sniffing butt, at least smart enough to stay away from the lowered antlers. In somewhat of a stupor from the heat, the elk remained on the ground, but swiveled his huge head trying to keep tabs on my excited dog. His eyes rolled back in his head, nostrils flaring. I finally got close enough to grab Keetna, apologized to the majestic beast, and dragged the dog back home.

One frosty winter's morning, we crunched through a couple of inches of snow up a hill. Upon reaching the crest, a bull elk emerged from the woods. Imperious in his winter finery as an emperor on

Coronation Day, the fur on his neck and mane were swaying from his run. He cocked his head over his back, eyes wild and rolling, snorting steam in small clouds. He turned towards us, and for a terrified moment I thought he was going to charge. Instead, he resumed his course, leaving nothing but his long stride of hoof prints in the snow. Emperors change their minds at will.

I was blessed to have the most beautiful workspace for eight years when I was the school librarian for Grand Canyon Schools. Floor to ceiling windows on the southeastern walls looked out onto the playground. I may be the only person in the world who has ever seen this—two young bull elk playing tag. I looked outside one day to see two gangly young elk chasing each other around the swing set. One raced madly in one direction, the other in pursuit. Abruptly, the lead elk turned around, lowering his antlers. The second elk now became the leader, racing to catch the rear end of the first elk. They continued this game for about twenty minutes, when I realized it was nearly time for recess. I had to call the office. "Better tell maintenance to clear the playground before the children emerge." I wonder if that was listed on the maintenance workers' job description – "chase elk off playground when necessary."

On a delightful walk behind my house, the San Francisco Peaks show cleanly between undulating hills covered with forest. In turning the other way and walking up a short hill, the Coconino Wall of the North Rim of the Grand Canyon is etched against the sky in the distance. One particular morning, my morning coffee caught up with me. Walking forward just enough to start down the other side of the hill, I finished my business, and stood from my squat to pull up my pants. Downhill from me, looking up with interest, were nine elk. They had not been there when I started my toilette. They were all at alert, ears straight up, noses pointing in my direction. When I stepped toward them, in unison they turned and ran downhill, white rumps bobbing, hooves pounding. Voyeurs. I thought I heard them laughing as they ran away.

On the trail out to Peaks View, I encountered a cow elk coming toward me. She threw back her head in surprise: looked at me wild-eyed, then lunged forward, gathering those long, springy legs under her so she could pivot north and flee. Her rhythmic pounding hooves continued to sound for a long time, hoof occasionally striking rock, my heart pounding with her until there was only the sound of the wind in the ponderosa needles.

Elk can run in short bursts up to 40 mph, and can maintain a steady run of 30 mph for longer distances. Elk are strong swimmers. One of their most impressive feats is being able to jump vertically from a standing position 8 to 10 feet straight up.

Historically, early explorers reported seeing an abundance of elk in Arizona, mainly in the White Mountains, although none were seen south of the Gila River. Elk habitat included most of today's United States, except for the Great Basin deserts and the Southern coastal plains. They survived the onslaught of pioneers better than the bison; their habitat in rough terrain protected them. However, in Arizona, the Merriam elk was hunted to extinction. Reports of large herds in the White Mountains were common throughout the 1870s, but by the 1880s, sightings were rare. This timeframe coincides exactly with the increased settlement in the Arizona Territory. Naturalist Edward W. Nelson sent two specimens of this elk native to Arizona back East, one in 1886 to the National Museum of Natural History in Washington, D.C., the other in 1887 to the American Museum of Natural History in New York. Thankfully he did, because other than a third specimen at the University of Arizona, there are no other Merriam elk recorded for posterity.

So, what are all these remaining elk we see in abundance in Northern Arizona? What follows is an interesting twist in man trying to make up for his mistakes.

By the early 1900s, it was clear that the elk population had subsided to the point of no return in Northern Arizona. Unregulated hunting had caused the elk to vanish from most of its former range, except for Yellowstone National Park. Our first national park had become a refuge for elk, causing its own set of problems. The introduction of livestock near the park had ousted the elk from their normal winter range, causing many elk to starve. Park officials began shipping live elk to other locales that had previously reported native elk herds. Dr. Robert Looney of Prescott, Arizona, contacted the Boone and Crockett Club of New York, whose mission was to restock animals for hunting to any part of the country where the native animals had been extirpated. A notable member of this organization was Theodore Roosevelt, the group's first president.

How to handle transporting wild animals thousands of miles? In February of 1913, the railroad moved everything in America. Arizona's first governor, George Hunt, a personal friend of Looney, helped to secure a permit to transport eighty elk from Yellowstone to Winslow, Arizona. The elk were captured and contained in Gardiner, Montana, just outside of Yellowstone National Park and then loaded onto boxcars for the long journey. Interestingly, although eighty elk went on the train in Yellowstone, 86 emerged from the boxcar in Winslow – 14 young bulls, 4 adult cows and 68 cow yearlings. And from these, you can see their descendants today.

Utterly exhausted upon arrival in Winslow, Arizona, the elk were allowed to rest before area sportsmen transported them in modified wool crates normally used by sheep men, with teams of horses pulling the bewildered elk. The elk were held in a corral near

Cabin Draw on Chevelon's Fork, some sixty-five miles south of Winslow. Watered and fed hay for two months, the elk were then released two months later when there was sufficient natural browse. The Elks Lodge of Arizona paid the $2500 for all costs incurred for this amazing experiment.

Two subsequent shipments were also successful, with 22 elk to south of Alpine in the Blue Range in 1927, and near Williams, Arizona, in 1928 with 54 elk.

So, how did these Yellowstone descendants extend their range and survive? The answer is simple – water. The abundant water sources in the White Mountains were the only perennial water elk could count on. As time went on and settlers obtained more livestock, cattle and sheep tanks proliferated throughout Arizona. The adaptable elk spread into areas that would have been too dry under natural conditions.

© Val Jesse

IV
Deer

Rare and otherworldly, fog is unfamiliar to Arizonans used to 9% humidity. It softens the needles of the ponderosa, blurs the images of buildings and cars, and tickles the nose. It's a Braille experience, like walking in a cotton-covered forest on my way to school. I sensed rather than saw movement before finding myself in the midst of a herd of deer. As if in understanding, they parted the herd and let me walk though, surrounded by alert ears and uplifted heads. They reformed their group, flowing back into the space they had let me borrow, honoring me with temporary membership in the herd.

In another encounter while I was walking Keetna, a herd of deer surprised us. I grabbed the dog and put her on leash. When I turned back to look, the deer, as if now sensing safety from attack, all seemed to float back into the forest. The forest was a mist cloud enfolding them, the deer just apparitions melting into the trees. Prey recognized predator and silently slipped away, vanishing into the trees in a timeless beauty.

Along the Colorado River, mule deer peek out coyly at the passing rafts from behind a tamarisk curtain along the river's edge. Surprising to see so many bucks, does, and yearlings considering the distance from their rim forests. Their oversized ears swivel toward us like SETI satellite dishes. It's a rough day – somewhere, I'm sure – but certainly not here watching deer along the river.

Up on the North Rim of the Grand Canyon, a heavy swath of clouds lay over the forest blanketing the North Kaibab Plateau. High beams from the car scarcely made a path. Luckily I knew every curve and bend in this road. Even so, landmarks loomed up suddenly. I slowed to round a turn and gasped at a herd of deer scattered across the road like an erratic chess game, eyes shining in the headlights. Slamming on the brakes wasn't going to be enough to avoid a catastrophe. There wasn't anything I could do. Powerless against the outcome, I let go of the wheel, prayed, and turned it over to the Goddess. Miraculously, the herd coalesced off to the left side of the road, and I sailed on through safely on the right. By the time I had passed through the herd, the car had finally come to a stop. I glanced in all rear view mirrors and couldn't see a single deer. They had all melted back into the forest and cloud cover like ghosts. But living ghosts.

Camping on the North Rim meant going out with a group of friends into the forest on some bumpy road leading off towards who-knew-where. It always involved beer, a campfire, and an incredible amount of storytelling and laughing. Afterwards, we'd toss out sleeping bags on pads and fall asleep to the wind ruffling the ponderosa needles. Upon waking after one such night, I opened my eyes to a sight that probably not many have seen – the underside of a male deer. His head lowered, he was eating a path around my sleeping bag. With the view I had, I was able to certify that indeed, this was a buck.

From a common Eurasian deer-like ancestor, all deer of North America entered this continent from Asia across the Bering land bridge five to six million years ago. After the mass extinction of the large ungulates such as camels, giant sloths, mastodons, and long-horned bison, deer moved in during the late Pleistocene (8,000-11,000 years ago) to fill these vacated ranges.

During the Pliocene, blacktails and whitetails diverged on the evolutionary tree of early deer-like forms. Mule deer became an offshoot of the blacktail branch, becoming larger in body and antler as they followed the line of receding glaciers. The word "mule" crept into the name of this deer because the size of its ears were similar to those of a mule, about 9½ inches long, not because of any genetic link to mules.

Early Native Americans, also fresh from Asia across the land bridge 13,000 years ago, hunted the prehistoric animals with Clovis points and atlatls. By around 4000-5000 years ago, after the die-off of the megafauna, bison, (albeit a smaller version) and deer assumed a greater significance to Native American hunters. The atlatl continued to be a primary weapon until around 1000 CE, when bows and arrows came into common usage. No doubt these improved the accuracy and effectiveness of deer hunting expeditions. Petroglyphs depicting hunters going after deer with these newfangled weapons coincide with archeologists noting an uptick in deer products used for clothing, tools, jewelry, ritual objects, and collections of antlers. These people were extremely resourceful, using every part of the deer, from sinew for bow strings, bones for awls, and antlers for scrapers. There was the obvious use of meat for food, and hides for clothing, sandals, arrow quivers and pouches. Hunting methods included ambush at a water source or experienced trackers following their quarry. The introduction of horses by the Spanish in the 1500s must have vastly improved deer hunting methodology, and facilitated the ease of bringing their prize back to camp.

Some of the first written descriptions of mule deer come from unlikely sources. Charles LeRaye was held captive by the Sioux tribe on the Big Sioux River in South Dakota, and noted these unusual deer in his field notes. Except for the backcountry of the national parks in the United States and Canada, none of the West looks the same as when Lewis and Clark first reported seeing mule deer on March 11, 1806.

The once abundant deer seriously declined as Anglo occupation spread. Unregulated hunting and the introduction of sheep and cattle in the 1870s negatively impacted the growth of mule deer herds. Also, drought plagued the West, and when the rains came, the stripped soil could not absorb it. Erosion was massive. Nothing could grow back. By the turn of the 20th century, deer herds were scarce.

Conservation strategies were slow to begin and often lax in restrictions and enforcement. Gradually scientists and game wardens learned that surplus males could be hunted without affecting the reproductive potential of the herd. Restrictions went into effect for the number of bucks to be culled, with permits being mandatory.

The debacle of attempted deer herd management on the Kaibab Plateau has been held up as a "don't do this" example. In the early

20th century, the government banned deer hunting on the Plateau, totally forgetting that Native Americans had lived and hunted on the Kaibab for millennia without causing a decimation of the deer herd. Next, the deer's predators, the mountain lions, coyotes, and bobcats, were hunted almost to extinction. In the case of wolves, complete eradication took place. The body count was appalling. The deer, freed from worry about predators, reproduced spectacularly, only to begin the process of starvation from lack of forage. Also, livestock consumed the browse deer could have eaten. Wily stockmen took advantage of the remoteness of the area by upping their cattle and sheep counts to beyond allotted levels. Once the grasslands were depleted, the overabundant cattle turned to woody plants, now competing directly with the deer. By 1923, portions of the normally verdant plateau were a dusty moonscape with scrawny deer gnawing on desperation forage.

A most humorous suggestion arose in 1924 to have a deer drive. 70 Navajos and 55 residents of the Arizona Strip attempted to herd deer to the edge of the canyon's North Rim, with plans to go down the Nankoweap Trail to the Colorado River, swim this huge herd across, and climb to the South Rim via the Tanner Trail, the old Horsethief Trail route. Unfortunately, horses and deer really only have their four legs in common, certainly not any herding instincts. Theoretically, thousands of deer should have been herded from rim to rim. In reality, there were more deer behind the drovers than in front of them. Not one deer cooperated with this experiment.

By 1929, Arizona Game and Fish established hunting regulations for deer kill season. The Forest Service tightened control over livestock owners. No predators were allowed to be taken. Slowly, conditions improved.

The lesson learned, like in so many other aspects of life, is that balance is crucial; in this case, balance between plants, plant-eaters, and their predators. Also learned — livestock grazing ruins the delicate landscape of the Southwest. One cow can eat six tons of vegetation per year, shuffling its heavy body through a landscape not adapted to that kind of hoof.

Besides obviously being a mammal, deer fall into the order of ungulates, meaning their highly developed toenails turn into hooves. Deer shed their antlers annually, putting them into the same category as moose, elk, caribou, and reindeer. The males shed last season's antlers between February and April. After a few weeks of allowing the pedicle wound – where the antlers were attached – to heal, new antlers begin to grow, up to a half-inch a day. In the summer, bachelor groups run together, while females hang around with other does and last year's fawns. By August, those antlers have reached full size and begin to harden. By September, the increase in testosterone in preparation for the rut causes the drying of the covering of velvet.

Bucks attack small trees or bushes to rub off the velvet, preparing their weapons. Interestingly, any injuries or abnormalities in one set of antlers tends to be repeated in any subsequent sets. Size of the rack tends to remain consistent year after year, too, and females take notice of this. All other traits being equal, the does go for the guy with the biggest (ahem) rack! Rival males become submissive in the presence of a buck with a bigger rack. This intimidation saves males from undue injury.

Mule deer range from Northern Mexico into New Mexico, Colorado, California, Nevada, Arizona, and Utah, along the Rocky Mountains, and up the coastal ranges into Canada. Mule deer are highly adaptable, and can live in ecozones ranging from 200 to 9000 feet in elevation.

Mule deer show alarm by a remarkable form of locomotion called stotting, when four hooves land and push off simultaneously, allowing them a fast getaway. Often after safely putting some distance between the cause of alarm and their new position, mule deer will pause and look back. A mule deer's eyes are on the sides of their heads, allowing almost a full circle (310°) of peripheral vision. Keenly aware of movement, they react by freezing or bolting, depending on the perceived danger. Their huge ears can swivel independently to evaluate strange sounds. Wind interferes with their hearing, causing them to be more skittish on breezy days. Their hearing range is similar to humans. Airborne scents also inform deer of danger.

Deer living in captivity, well-cared for and well-fed can live between 15-20 years. In the wild, the average is closer to 13 years. Deer teeth can be used like tree rings; annual rings form on the tooth's interior and can be counted to determine the deer's age.

V
Bighorn Sheep

I told my aunt about the new, two-story, composting outhouse at Cedar Ridge, strongly recommending the use of the top floor. She laughed and laughed, and said she'd like a picture of that. So, there I was, heading down the South Kaibab Trail, camera at the ready.

A scattering of stones sliding downwards stopped me on the trail. A bighorn sheep with huge curled horns clattered down the cliff face above me. Landing on the trail in front of me with a thump and a shake, he approached. I drew out my camera and fired off several shots, then paused to admire his horns before realizing he wasn't going to yield to a mere human. I scrambled upslope to get out of his way, and he passed right by me. At the next switchback he abandoned the trail and went right over the edge. I ran after him and watched him pick his way with an air of insouciance down a 90° angle before finding a narrow ledge to traverse to the next layer.

Bighorn are common enough along the river. One memorable sighting was a ewe and her lamb on a tight ledge right over the Colorado River. As our rafts floated along, the ewe watched us, but quickly lost interest and returned to gnawing on the sagebrush. The lamb, however, was enthralled, watching us head toward and sail under that ledge, and it obviously wanted to continue watching. But the ledge was so tight, and with mama's rump right there, it couldn't turn around. So, in nosy desperation, it stuck its little head under and between its legs, and watched us upside down until we were out of sight.

I have been close enough to see their odd eyes with the pupil going eerily sideways, to see a puff of breath through their nostrils on a cold winter day on the Bright Angel Trail. My husband, Keith was a ranger for 21 years. He has his own bighorn story. Keith shares it here.

> I was a ranger on the South Rim of Grand Canyon. My favorite program was a guided hike down the South Kaibab Trail to Cedar Ridge, a one and a half mile hike

1,500 feet down into the canyon. I started the hike at 7:30 that morning and ended at Cedar Ridge around 10 a.m.

Walking the trail back up out of the canyon in a ranger uniform took some time because I had to stop and talk to everybody I met along the way. It was nearly noon when I approached "The Chimney," a set of switchbacks near the top of the trail.

I approached a group of hikers waiting at the bottom of the switchbacks. They said they couldn't go farther because a desert bighorn sheep blocked the trail. Also, there was a crowd at the trailhead that couldn't come down for the same reason. These people were glad to see me, a ranger, because I could certainly get that scary bighorn off the trail.

I wasn't sure what to do. I walked up the trail to a place just before it turned back on itself a little higher up. When my eyes got up to the level of the trail on the next switchback, I found myself staring face-to-face at a desert bighorn lying on the trail.

It didn't move, so I began talking to it and then screaming at it. The bighorn continued looking at me with curiosity. I was using two walking sticks. I waved them over my head and continued screaming, "Come on, get up. You can't stay here!" I couldn't quite touch him so I pounded on the ground in front of him with my walking sticks. Slowly he got up.

"Now we're getting someplace," I thought, but all the bighorn did was walk toward me and start licking the end of my walking sticks, showing just how scary we rangers can be.

Eventually, a Student Conservation Association (SCA) volunteer ranger hiked up from behind, emboldening me to get up the switchback to the same level as the bighorn. By this time, the bighorn had laid back down again.

The SCA ranger and I stood side by side, waving our hands in the air to look even more menacing, and marched forward making as much noise as possible. The bighorn, rather resignedly, got up and wandered over to the outside edge of the trail. He gave us one last baleful look and then leaped over the edge down a six-foot cliff to the next switchback below, bounded across the trail and down another ten feet to the next switchback, and then off that one onto the eighty-degree slope of the canyon wall. He was gone.

Not all of my encounters were with live sheep. The bighorn are also honored in death. Four rams had given up their sacred lives to poachers within the boundary of the Havasupai Nation. A ceremony had been created as a healing for these animals so senselessly slaughtered. On the South Rim of the Grand Canyon at the Shrine of the Ages, we waited, this packed audience of more than 250 people. Feet shuffled, coughs muted behind hands, pieces of paper flapped before faces flushed with the July heat. From the back of the room came the sound of tinkling bells followed by the deep rhythm of a bass drum. Heads swiveled as the Guardians of the Canyon danced into view. Havasupai emerged in a straight line in full ceremonial regalia. Four tribesmen wore the curved ram horns of the bighorn sheep. Turkey feathers hung down from red headbands, shielding the ram dancers' faces. In one hand, each held a carved walking stick, in the other a rattle decorated with pine boughs. Painted buckskin loincloths were tied over leggings with woven red belts. Exposed chests were painted chalky white. Women, magnificent in their long fringed buckskin dresses with hooves hung from their belts as rattles, danced between the ram dancers. Colorful capes representing the myriad colors of sunset were draped over the women's backs and shoulders. Some hair was braided with vivid ribbons of black, yellow and red while another had a small burden basket dangling from her ponytail. Chanters joined in, matching their rhythm with the drum's heartbeat. The line danced its way onto the stage, joined together in a circle, expanding and contracting the circle with small and then larger footsteps. The flow of the dancers' circle continued around and around, forward and backward, drawing the audience into the

flow of life in the Grand Canyon. The dancers left the stage, circled the auditorium, and then retreated. The chanters ended their verse, drumbeats quieted and then stopped altogether. For a moment, phantom echoes of the song and drum reverberated throughout the silent room. The dancers reminded us that we are all one. What happens to one being can happen to others. Who better to teach us than the Havasupai Tribe, those who have lived their lives in the center of the Grand Canyon as their ancestors did for centuries before us?

Unmistakable with its curved ram horns, the bighorn sheep is the most depicted figure on the rock walls of the Southwest. They crossed the Bering Strait land bridge from Eurasia, arriving about the same time as human migrants. These wild sheep most likely originated from Siberian stock in isolation among the glaciers, making this species ill-equipped to fight diseases from today's domestic stock.

The home of bighorns is spectacular: remote, dangerous, other-worldly. Rugged landscapes are their favorite haunts, the more precipitous the better. Seeking shelter in caves and overhangs, rocks are scraped away for their bedding-down areas. Ancient layers of droppings prove the herd memory of these safe places. Elevationally speaking, bighorns can comfortably live from 200 feet to 7000 feet above sea level.

Sheep have amber eyes and excellent vision. A herd selects a sentinel ram as lookout, but he pays more attention to what is below rather than above. Predators, both human and animal, seriously contemplating a bighorn dinner, have learned to approach sheep from above. Bobcats, mountain lions, and coyotes are the biggest threat to bighorns. Lambs are vulnerable to attack from golden eagles and foxes.

Their average lifespan is 10-14 years, but an occasional sheep has made it to 20. Somewhat along the line of tree rings, age can be determined in rams by counting the cross-ridge rings on their horns, each being approximately a year. Bighorns keep their horns for life and do not shed them.

Other than a few grunts, snorts, bleats or blats, bighorns are fairly quiet creatures. Occasionally they grind their teeth to show increasing agitation. Desert bighorns pant nosily like dogs and also perspire to disperse body heat.

Rams are opportunists who wait for receptive ewes in estrous and mate, then look around for another partner. Check out a ram's testicles—they are impressively huge considering the size of the animal. There is a lot of posturing and horn display to attract the ewes and establish dominance. Sometimes these episodes of "Mine's bigger" escalate into armed conflict. And, boy howdy, do they ever have armament. Their horns alone can weigh thirty pounds. A dramatic charge may occur with both males raising their front legs and falling toward each other's horns in a loud head-cracking blow, the sound bouncing and echoing between canyon walls. The fight ends if a contestant stumbles and falls.

Desert bighorn sheep are found in Utah, New Mexico, Nevada, Arizona, West Texas, California, Colorado, and Mexico. They are the most vulnerable population of bighorn sheep due to the extremes of their environment and the encroachment of humans on their already limited habitat.

Bighorns were the equivalent of the bison herds as the main food animal of the desert Southwest for early Native Americans. The sheep's parts were used for clothing, tools, spoons, ladles, and water containers. That big horn can hold a gallon of water. The extremely strong hide was used to make braided ropes for negotiating cliff faces by rappelling and belaying. The grease of the bighorn was highly prized and was used for everything from hair adornment to medicinal uses. Havasupai hunters wore a ewe's hide covered in ashes trying to attract a ram.

Native American cosmology describe the stars as the Mountain Sheep in what we call the constellation Orion. The three stars in the belt are the sheep, with the sword or dagger of today being the stone-tipped arrow of the Ancient Ones.

Shoshones place the head of a sheep away from their camp, facing east, so the sun can greet the deceased and help to regenerate its spirit for future successful hunts. Lakota use the ram's horns to transfer ceremonial fire.

Lewis and Clark described various bands of Indians that commonly ate the sheep, especially in what is now Montana. They documented sighting Audubon's sheep, a species of bighorn extirpated as early as 1916. Charles Sheldon, an avid hunter of bighorn, reported in December of 1913 observing their impressive foraging of saguaros. They attack the giant cactus by butting against the base with their horns, helping to crush those pesky spines. Chewing all the way around a saguaro four to five feet off the ground, they search for water. Records show bighorns getting as deep as six inches into the trunk in this manner, looking for water and cactus juice as a form of carbohydrate. Head-butting the saguaro to dislodge fruit is another bighorn tactic. Sheldon noted this on his trip to the Arizona/Sonora border, where the desert bighorn survive on ephedra, cholla, and prickly pear for lunch.

There is a story from Ellen Meloy's magnificent book about bighorns, *Eating Stone*. A desert mountain lion in the harsh environment along the California/Mexico border was found dead from malnutrition. But there was also evidence that it had killed and eaten thirteen desert bighorn sheep. Talk about lean meat.

Desert bighorn sheep populations continued a slow slide toward extinction in the early 1900s. Encroachment on their environment by prospectors, miners, settlers, and Indians excited to try out their newly acquired guns certainly contributed to the bighorn's decline. But the real reason was unknown to scientists of that time. Exposure to livestock diseases was just as catastrophic to the bighorns as European diseases were to the Native Americans. In addition to disease, competition for the same forage as the numerous domestic sheep, goats, cattle, burros, and horses was just too much for the shy bighorns. A combination approach helped to save the bighorns: reasonable and strict hunting regulations, and the formation of protected game ranges, national monuments, state parks, wildlife refuges, and recreation areas. All are sanctuaries for bighorns with no hunting and no intrusions of domestic stock. The 2,660,000-acre Barry M. Goldwater Gunnery Range in southern Arizona is closed to livestock, creating a haven in the Tinajas Atlas Range for the bighorn. Mexico has also created national parks along the Sonoran border that benefit bighorn.

I look forward to the next time I'm alone on the Kaibab Trail and hear an unexpected avalanche of stones clattering downwards. The thrill of seeing a desert bighorn silhouetted above the ridgeline makes it worth the hard hike just to see that again.

VI
Coyote

Some encounters would make good Arizona postcards. On one of my many work trips on the Colorado River with Arizona Raft Adventures (AZRA), somewhere in the Redwall, we saw him, a magnificent coyote trotting upriver in that easy, ground-covering lope, a huge rabbit dangling from his jaws. The colors of his fur were gorgeous—auburn golden, dipped in chocolate at the tips, with a luxurious bushy tail.

Such snapshots sometimes invite a closer look. On the day after Winter Solstice, I took my dog Keetna out for a hike to celebrate the return of the light. As we were heading back, Keetna stopped and looked intently up the ridge. Following her gaze, I saw a coyote watching us. I grabbed Keetna and put her back on leash. The coyote looked down at us, while we gazed up at it on the ridgeline. Then the coyote did an astonishing thing…it lay down. Keetna and I crept forward for a closer look, finally getting too close. So he got up and headed away. The coyote repeated this three times, picking his way through boulders, downed logs and winter-dried grasses, always keeping his wary eyes on us, until disappearing from sight over the top of the ridge. Reluctantly, we broke the spell and headed home. But, high and far away, from over canyons and cliffs, we heard a cry, a farewell and thanks. What a thrilling and life-affirming event to remind us that the light is now on its return cycle, and that spring is on the way.

One cold day as autumn tried to transform itself into winter, I crouched near the pond to pee. When I stood up, I saw movement between me and the aspen grove. A small coyote brushed a path through the tall grass. I stood up on the railroad ties for a better view when she saw me. From her position, I must have sprung out of the dirt. She watched me warily, then loped off to the middle of the meadow, leaving plenty of space between us, pausing in her stride to swivel her head toward me. I stood statue-still, only my eyes moving to watch her pick her way through the tall, dead grass. Overhead, a red-tailed hawk circled, whistling. When the coyote was far enough away from me for her comfort level, she broke into a run.

In the forest about a mile south of our Grand Canyon apartment, Keetna suddenly bolted and ran ahead to something in the grass. As I got closer, I saw to my horror, two coyote pups. I grabbed Keetna back before she could make contact, and out from the forest charged Mama, barking and growling furiously. The babies understood Mama's orders, and hightailed it far back into the woods away from that scary dog and human. Next, Mama Coyote sat down about thirty feet away from us, rather self-composed, I thought, and seemed to be thinking about the meaning of life, nose in the air, sniffing. After a long wait, Mama loped off in the direction of the disappeared pups. Stopping, she threw back her head and howled, a long, undulating note of pure wild. From far away came little yips, which became louder and closer together as the babies scampered toward the sound of their Mama's howl. What a greeting we witnessed, noses rubbing, tails wagging, Mama licking each one carefully, making sure everybody was just fine. Mama gave one baleful glance in the direction of Keetna and me, then trotted off to the west, little ones very close to her heels.

Often, both at Grand Canyon and other remote locations, I wake up to the sound of a coyote. It's still a thrill, no matter how many times I hear it. The pack communicating about a target prey, the celebration of a kill, or just a solitary being exclaiming its joy to the Universe—it's the sound of the wild.

Coyotes evolved right here on this continent. Three to twelve million years ago, dire wolves were the top dog in North America. They only ate large herbivores, presenting a problem when those started to die out. Small, fox-like creatures didn't have such a restricted diet; they ate any small thing that moved, and some that didn't, like fruits and nuts. When the 175-pound dire wolves died out, the smaller canids, ancestors of today's wolves, coyotes, and foxes, were waiting to fill in. The earliest coyote fossil dating back to the Ice Age was found in Maryland. Today's coyotes have found ways to adapt, pushing their range across the continent and down into Central America, even showing up in New York City and other urban areas.

The scientific name for coyote is *Canis latrans* or "barking dog." Its howl is unforgettable and lingers in the air long after the snout has closed. Aztecs provided the root for the word coyote, from Coyolxauhaui, a moon goddess, her name meaning "bayer-at-the-moon."

The desert coyote's ability to adapt has served him well. Lush fur fits nicely in their habitat. All coats include variegated colors of tawny, cream, rust, brown, yellow and black, making a striking coat up close. Their yellow eyes give a glimpse into their canny intelligence, which has helped them survive. Coyotes are long-range purposeful lopers, roaming from 25 to 400 miles in search of food. Coyotes eat almost anything, but their preference is carnivorous. Hungry coyotes turn vegetarian if they have to.

Coyotes form a pack mostly for the raising of pups. A loosely organized family group consists of the current mated pair and their pups, litters ranging from four to six, a couple of last year's pups, and some aunts, uncles, or grandparents, who may or may not be actual blood relations.

Coyotes tend to hunt alone or in pairs rather than in packs like wolves. The oddest hunting partners are a coyote and a badger. Yep, it's been observed. When the fast digging badger goes into a rodent's hole, there's usually a back door. An alert coyote watches and waits, and then pounces on whatever comes racing out of the exit. Many Native American stories feature Coyote and Badger together.

Hopi and Navajo coyote tales hold surprisingly similar plot lines, proving the intertwining of tribal relations over time. Navajos, more centered around hunting, portray Coyote to be a demonic, witchy, god-figure. The agricultural Hopis take Coyote more as a harmless fool.

Coyote in storytelling has been known as a horn dog lecher with a long penis. He's also seen as a gullible dupe with the other animals constantly tricking him. Crow can pretend to chop off his leg, convincing Coyote to really chop off his. Badger pretends to remove his own intestines, and convinces Coyote to really remove his. Turkey Woman pretends to kill her own children and then magically return them to the living. Then she's extremely glad when Coyote Woman really kills her own children, thus saving the turkey chicks from predation, but leaving the grief-stricken Coyote howling over the loss of her pups. Coyote wants to copy everyone, and even better—go one above whatever anyone else is doing. Only a few tales see Coyote emerge as a hero, such as when Coyote faced an ogre to help free some captive children. Coyote was also the hero for bringing the Kachinas to Walpi, who in turn gave the villagers life-saving seeds.

But mostly, Coyote plays the fool. Once, watching a flock of blue jays, she noticed the birds fly up, release an object and then swoop down to catch it. Time and time again, the flock played this game. Finally one blue jay landed close enough that Coyote could ask what the game was. Blue Jay explained that one bird would take out someone's eye; the flock would chase after it, then give it back to the owner. Coyote, of course, not to be outdone, took out both of her eyes. Two birds flew up, each holding an eye, while the rest of the flock lifted Coyote into the air. From high up, the birds released the eyes and all the jays screeched, pointing out the location of the falling eyes. Poor Coyote couldn't understand the yelling birds, and the eyes plummeted right past her to the ground. The flock brought her back to Earth, and she blindly groped around, failing to find her eyes. The jays pulled some sap from a tree, stuffing it where her eyes had been. And that's why coyotes have yellow eyes today.

Lewis and Clark were among the first whites to report seeing coyotes in 1805. Coyotes spread widely to escape predators and take advantage of the prairies and edges near forest depletion. Now their range is the largest in this hemisphere save that of humans. Fewer predators, combined with the coyote's adaptability, have helped expand its presence, despite campaigns to eradicate it. Coyotes moving north and east were sparse, and came across the even more rare last remnants of wolf packs. Although cross-species interbreeding is uncommon, coyote/wolf hybrids began showing up in New England in the 1930s and '40s. Pictures clearly show the differences between the more slender, angular western coyote, and the stockier, broader eastern coyote. The eastern variety shows its ties to wolf ancestry by preferring forested areas, hunting larger prey in packs, and is more social than the western, more fox-like coyote. Living up to their wily reputations, coyotes have an array of defense mechanisms. They carry their tails down, their ears up and are ever alert—a key difference from domestic dogs. Coyote's sense of smell is his strongest asset, capable of sniffing out targets a mile away

Their perky, always alert ears can tune into rodent activity underground. Another defense is wariness. Anything that looks out of place is cause for intense observation. Howls can be heard from over three miles away, making it devilishly difficult to determine where the sound is coming from. With the sound echoing off rocky ridges and hillsides, it magnifies what might just be a mated pair with a couple of pups into sounding like a dozen. Howling can proclaim territory to prevent injurious fighting, or to announce a kill. It can be a way of calling the troops together. Or, it could just be a joyous expression of being alive in the wilderness, free.

Coyotes are exceptional parents, devoted to each other for at least that breeding season, and often longer, which is more than can be said about some humans.

Urban coyotes are truly the wiliest of coyotes, living in open green spaces like parks, cemeteries, and airports. One pilot noted a coyote on the runway when he left Texas, and one upon landing in Ohio, too. The most famous airport coyote story took place at the Portland, Oregon, airport. Officials chased a coyote off the runway, and Wily E. Coyote jumped on a light rail train headed for downtown, scoring a window seat. After that excitement, he was successfully captured and relocated to the wild. Oh, the howls he could tell about that adventure. Coyotes have also wandered into other bizarre locales – a sandwich shop in Chicago, a furniture store in Kansas, an elevator in Seattle, a house in Massachusetts, and a turnpike toll booth in Boston. City dwellers should be grateful for coyotes, who gorge on rats.

Coyote as Trickster, even sometimes as an animal god, can be silly, foolish, heroic, a bestower of fortune, or a trouble maker. These stories of coyote's traits serve as reminders of what it is to be human, as all of us play these different roles at times.

The Yakima use Coyote and Eagle powerfully in the story of their journey to the Land of the Dead. Eagle's wife dies, and he begs his friend Coyote to travel with him to the Land of the Dead to bring her back. They have to cross a river filled with spirits of the dead. Coyote's howl stuns the spirits so Eagle can grab his wife's spirit and put it in a bag and return her to the Land of the Living. But as dawn breaks, the canoe overturns, and her spirit flees. Because, you see, life and death are equal halves, one cannot pilfer from the other. And someday you'll be taken to the Land of the Dead and stay there forever.

Because of his remarkable adaptability, the coyote has survived attempts of eradication and has lived to tell these tales.

VII
Fox

A lot of action takes place on our woodsy driveway. One night, our headlights offered a glimpse of something too small to be a coyote, too sleek and elegant to be a raccoon. A fox? Perhaps.

In another driveway appearance, a grey fox flashed in front of the car, then stepped behind a fallen log to peer back at me, our curiosity mutual. I lowered the car window and stopped, enchanted by the creature's beauty, the cat-like way it sat on its haunches and gazed back at me. Curling its beautiful grey bushy tail around its paws, it looked like a dowager countess flinging a foxtail scarf across her shoulders. The ears remained perked up, alert. I drove off slowly, glancing back. The fox followed the car's progress with swiveled head before ambling into the woods, neither of us anxious to let go.

Another time though, I was on foot as the fox appeared. My mind replayed all the rabid fox stories I have heard, but this animal seemed composed and curious. It was far enough away from me to be safe for both of us, but close enough for observation – graceful and sleek, it had a long black stripe running from its haunches to the tip of that bushy tail. Then, it started toward me. "Oh, no you don't, you stay right there," I said in my best teacher voice. Surprisingly, it sat down. As soon as I was out of range, it ran back down the cliff. As always, these encounters are brief and end in our leaving in separate directions, reluctantly so, on my part. Hmmmm. I wonder if there's a den down there.

Later, from my deck, I pulled out some binoculars and scanned our two-acre property near the cliff face where the fox had disappeared. To my astonishment, a baby fox came tumbling out from between some boulders and logs. Soon, a second followed, then a third and fourth. So began our devotion to Fox News—and thankfully, it had nothing to do with television.

Some sightings are more graphic than others. On one occasion an adult fox arrived with the body of a rabbit in its jaws, legs and ears dangling. In a sweeter moment, we watched Mama nursing, the kits shoving and bumping to get closer, one doing a limbo move to get under her. She took it stoically for a while, then jumped to a log above the den to get away from that rambunctious bunch. Afternoons tended to be just the kits, the adults away hunting. The kits chased each other round and round, occasionally trying out their tree climbing skills on the ponderosas closest to the den opening. Once, one baby lay flat out on the ground, tummy down in the warm dirt, all four legs stretched out to form an X. A sibling tumbled over it, stomping that resting head right into the ground. The dazed little one stood up, shaking its head for a while. Impossibly cute. Pouncing, skittering, jumping, and scampering are all words for fox family antics. When an adult returned, it was quite the welcome home scene. Noses rubbed, playful paw swipes meted out, and lots of jostling. Evenings continued the antics, those kits were non-stop action.

We had all our meals on the deck, binoculars at the ready, so when I spied movement I could describe all of the activity to my blind husband Keith. The foxes seemed quite content in their den area, with an adult occasionally staring intently toward the deck. I don't think the babies ever caught on that mesmerized humans watched their every move.

But one morning all that changed. We heard barking, that odd, hoarse coughing sound of a fox. One adult raced past our house to the north yelping, the other adult barked and headed south. The kits disappeared. The cause of all this commotion was soon apparent – a beat-up looking coyote loped down the dirt road below our house. After watching the delicate, sophisticated foxes for so long, this coyote looked like a surly brute, perhaps a bouncer at a forest dive. Although the adult foxes frantically tried to act as decoys luring it away from the den, the coyote was having none of that. He made a straight path toward the den. Nightgown flapping, I ran toward it. This bruiser wasn't going to hurt those precious kits. The coyote, nonplussed by my appearance, nosed around the den area, then strutted off down the road. The kits remained burrowed deep for hours.

We watched the den that whole afternoon. Nothing moved. Later one of the adults ran below the cliff under our house, barking, heading straight toward the den. There was a frantic reunion as the kits emerged writhing and jumping. Then the sun set and shut down our view of the action for the night.

But, it was obvious the next day what had transpired. With their security breached, the whole family had moved out under the cover of darkness, leaving no forwarding address. They were gone, vanished into the trackless wilderness of the Kaibab National Forest. Should we all be so lucky to watch this kind of Fox News.

When Keith was a park ranger at Walnut Canyon National Monument, we had the privilege of living in one of the rock houses built by the Civilian Conservation Corps in the 1930s. Keith's summers were busy working, but as a teacher, I got to loll around for a few months. One of my favorite walks was to an old ranger cabin, fallen into disrepair, slated for restoration once funding became available.

Resting against an old-growth ponderosa, musing about what it must have been like 100 years ago when the ranger cabin was new, I saw a fox wriggle out from beneath the dilapidated structure—perfect den site for a mother red fox. Out of the way, human smell quite faint and old, the broken wooden floor provided a roof and a good place to burrow. I often sat back a ways in the woods and waited to see if she emerged for a hunt. Early mornings were the best time for action. There were at least two kits, little balls of fluff.

One time Mama left, and after a slight delay, a tiny nose poked out of the hole and followed her. Mama must have had her intuition set on high that day, as the little one didn't get very far before Mama came charging back. She uttered a short little bark, which could be interpreted by exasperated mothers everywhere as "Where do you think you're going?" And then, picking it up by the scruff of its neck, she hustled it back into the burrow. One could almost hear her sigh when she once again exited the hole to resume her hunt.

While a fox weighs about five pounds, its favorite breakfast, jackrabbit, can weigh up to ten pounds. The fox can accomplish this because of its stealthy and incredibly fast run. It needs to be fast, because its prey includes ducks, birds, and small burrowing animals. Also like cats, its front claws are retractable, great for grabbing and holding onto scurrying prey. A fox can lunge seventeen feet in the air to pin prey to the ground. Other foodstuffs don't require as much gymnastics, as a fox will also eat wild fruit, corn, and insects. Their diet changes from habitat to habitat, season to season, always preferring rabbits when available. Fox are experts at hiding and caching food for future use, their stomachs too small to gorge as a wolf can. Their hearing is keenly tuned into listening for underground maneuverings of their dinner. A fox can hear a mouse move under two feet of snow. Pretty amazing to be able to conquer prey only heard, not seen. Preferring dawn and dusk hunting expeditions, foxes mirror the activity of their prey. They tend to favor downhill hunting, rushing their prey from a ridgeline or atop a boulder.

Foxes need 25 acres to 40 square miles of territory in order to survive, depending on the lushness of their environment. Fox prefer habitat along the edges of forests and meadows. Patchwork pastures, dense with shrubbery, are perfect for small rodents and rabbits to hide. At about three and a half months, the parents severely reduce the amount of food brought to the den to lure the kits out to find food on their own. The young fox dines first on insects and berries, gradually moving on to meatier prey. Male kits leave the family territory by October, while some of the female kits, or vixens, stay on and help raise the next generation in the spring.

Foxes adapt differently to different environments. Desert foxes need the most adaptations to their stark habitat: large ears for heat dispersion, the ability to utilize food as a water source, multiple dens to hide from the sun and wind, and dark eyes to help protect against the solar glare.

Moving from desert to forest, we discover a tree-climbing fox. Grey foxes can climb trees. The grey fox chooses to spend most of it time in a forest environment, so it more readily takes the high road than the red fox. Climbing straight up like a bear, this agile fox can also hop from branch to branch.

Red foxes show more color variety – from red to amber with a tinge of orange, and a black stripe running down the back to its bushy tail. The tip of the tail is all black.

It's their gorgeous fur that caused massive trapping of these magnificent creatures. Poison and flagrant hunting, most notably with dogs, made a huge dent in the fox population. But adaptable and stealthy, foxes never became an endangered species.

Although the red fox and the grey fox overlap in choices of habitat, they do not overlap in DNA. The distinctly separate family tree of the grey fox branched out four to six million years ago. Ranging from southern Canada to northern Venezuela, the smaller grey fox can be found anywhere except extreme mountainous areas or on the Great Plains.

And I would love to again find another one denning nearby.

VIII
Grizzly Bear

After years of living in Grand Canyon National Park, we were
used to elk jams and deer jams. But in Grand Teton National Park,
this was grizzly bear gridlock. Two cars ahead of us, a magnificent
male strutted across the meadow, paws slightly pigeon-toed. On all
fours, his head could look over the hood of a SUV. His fur rippled
with each step, shining auburn, his 4-inch claws picking up the
sunlight with each step. Walking steadily to the road, he crossed it
without breaking stride, not even glancing at the gawking tourists.

During a fabulous adventure on a Lindblad ship in Alaska's
Inside Passage, we often stopped to hike on uninhabited islands.
For safety, we always traveled in groups of five or six, making lots of
noise to avoid surprising a bear, a serious breach of grizzly etiquette.
Two groups circumnavigated the island in opposite directions for
minimal impact, observing flora and fauna along the way. Naturalist
guides led each group, with a hyper-alert volunteer bringing up
the rear, scanning for bears. Our leader also had a bear bell on her
bracelet, which kept up a rhythmic clanging as we hiked. Keith was
#5 in our line, and I was the #6 watcher on guard at the end. Dense
vegetation lined the trail along a stream teeming with salmon. At
the half-way point we encountered the other group. Their leader
pointed to the ground, frowning. The object of his concern was
a big, steaming pile of bear poop. "That was not here when we
came the other way," he said. "Everyone stay close together and be
extremely watchful."

Our groups continued in opposite directions. The trees and
plants closed in on us, so that I could hardly see the woman in front
of Keith. Suddenly our guide erupted in a series of whoops and
hollers, with everyone in line ahead joining in. I heard a huge splash
in the stream. Finally a break in the vegetation allowed me to see
the tail end of an enormous grizzly splashing across the creek to the
opposite side, away from these noisy hikers. Considering we were

only a stream-width apart, I was grateful to get a safe close-up of THAT end of a grizzly. In retreat.

A grizzly male weighs between 1000 and 1500 pounds, is nine and a half feet long and four and a half feet tall at that humped shoulder. They will sometimes kill and eat the cubs. Who's going to stop them? Certainly not the females, who can stand 8 feet tall but weigh only 500 pounds. Yet, bears have the smallest babies in relation to the size of the mother's body. If the ratio were the same in humans, a newborn human would weigh six ounces. Bears can plow through dense underbrush like a tank. And, during courtship, the male approaches the female with all the delicacy of a runaway locomotive. A single swipe of the male's paw can fell a moose, elk, or caribou, or rearrange a 200-pound boulder.

Bears can smell across a thousand-yard body of water to notice when another bear is present, using a sense of smell seven times more powerful than that of a bloodhound. They can pick up a human scent from two miles away. Speaking of smell, the only animal known to cause a bear to beat a hasty retreat is a skunk. Brown bears and grizzlies are the same species. Grizzly bears live only in the upper tier of North America, whereas brown bears reside across the world.

Grizzlies were formerly common in Arizona. Frederick Dellenbaugh reported grizzly tracks on John Wesley Powell's second expedition along the Colorado River in 1871-72. The densest population of grizzly bears resided around Sitgreaves Mountain at approximately one bear per acre. That's the mountain I see from my deck, which would sure have changed my hiking habits. When the grizzlies were extirpated from Arizona, black bears moved in to fill the void.

Today's populations of grizzlies in the Lower 48 reside in our national parks, specifically Yellowstone, Grand Teton, and Glacier. Alaska is still our final frontier, as well as for the grizzly.

During the salmon runs, grizzlies catch as many as 50 fish per day. One record breaking bear was observed catching 89 fish in ten hours. Before hibernation, bears eat up to 90 pounds of food per day, or about 20,000 calories. After hibernation, bears may lose up to one third of their body weight. Clearly, I need to hibernate.

Female bears are the only mammal which gives birth in the dead of winter during hibernation. I'm sure there are human mothers who would sign up for that way of giving birth.

The deciding factor for hibernation is not about weather, but rather the availability of food. Approximately half the year is spent in hibernation. No food or drink is required during denning time. Thus there is no need for elimination, making for a much tidier den.

There is a greater chance of being struck by lightning than being attacked by a bear. There has never been a recorded attack on a group of three or more people. The grizzly rules are simple—don't come between a food source and/or the cubs. A standing bear is not getting ready to charge, but rather is nervous and wants to check things out.

Fifteen million years ago during the Pleistocene, short faced bears were the largest predator on the planet, males weighing up to a ton. Archeological records show this bear existed at the same time as early Native Americans. Just imagine! The short faced bear disappeared with the last Ice Age due to climate change and human encroachment. Lessons we can learn, perhaps, from a keystone species such as the grizzly?

So, where do grizzlies hail from? A new bear arose in Eurasia, evolving into the modern brown bear about 1.6 million years ago. Crossing into Alaska 50,000-70,000 years ago, it crossed paths with our human ancestors, competing for the same basic food and shelter requirements.

Bears are held in high regard by all ancient societies that encountered them. Because of their unusual habit of hibernation, bears are seen as communicators with the spirit world. As far back as 50,000 years ago, Neanderthals created an altar in a cave in Switzerland with seven bear skulls facing the cave entrance. Petroglyphs in France from 30,000 years ago show two men dancing with a bear.

Both the Greeks and the Inuit – two cultures that never interacted – placed their bear myths in the same constellations. Many traditions say in star lore that the Great Bear, also known as the Big Dipper, sinks low in the sky in autumn, looking for a place to hibernate. Many legends tell of bears as fur-clad people, able to slip in and out of their coats to mingle with the people. The Ojibwa use the same word for people and bears. Navajo and Cree use the honorific word Chief for bear. Yavapai say that bears are like people except they can't make fire. Queen Hatshepsut of Egypt kept bears in 1500 BCE. As far back as the Romans, bears were used for zoos and gladiatorial combat. This continued as late as 1880 in California with bears being pitted against bulls. The city of Bern, capital of Switzerland along the Aare River, has had a bear pit in the city center since 1441.

When Lewis and Clark ventured into the remote mountain ranges and high plateaus of what is now Montana and North Dakota, they encountered grizzlies almost daily. With grizzlies able to go 0-40 mph for a mile or more, the expedition members must have been sprinting like Olympians. Even at that, the bear could still outrun them, dispelling the myth of the heavy, slow moving bear.

The Great Mail Theft of 1929 occurred in Yellowstone National Park. The mail carrier left the truck windows open on a warm summer's day. A bear swiped the mailbag out of the truck and climbed a tree. Shuffling through the mail, the bear opened and devoured a box of chocolate chip cookies. The bear then went through the mail a second time, and not finding anything else, dropped the bag and took a nap in the tree.

All the rest of the numerous grizzly bears I've seen were on a shoreline, and I was safely on a ship to appreciate these magnificent creatures from a respectful distance.

©ValJesse

IX
Mountain Lion

Ghost cat. Shadow cat. Glimpses. I guess I've been lucky. I've had four personal encounters with mountain lions and heard one scream.

Driving away from Desert View Tower on the South Rim at dusk, I spot a loping female stretched out across the road, perfectly silhouetted against the sinking sun. In one fast-forward move she rose and leaped, her long legs churning, ropey tail straight out behind her for balance. It all happened so fast only people in the front seat saw it—the back seat passengers never had a chance.

It was lightly raining near Hell's Canyon as I headed to Walnut Canyon to spend the weekend with Keith, no other cars on that rain-slick road. Off the high eastern cliff, even faster than suddenly, a mountain lion launched itself. It hit the double yellow line with all paws as I hit the brakes and skidded to a stop right where the cougar had been, now just a piece of wet road. In one giant leap for cat-kind, it sprang from the yellow line to half-way up the western wall. Then it bounded to the ridgeline and disappeared over the top, faster than any high tech camera could ever capture.

Patagonia-Sonoita Creek Sanctuary. Lush, leafy riparian plants, forests dense with willows and cottonwoods all lining this sparkling creek in southern Arizona. We stopped to inhale the perfume of all this vegetation. Not a breath of wind. Then, twenty feet ahead of us, the bushes and grasses began to rustle and move, a dry land river with a current. From out of the plant matter rose a ropey brown tail with a black tip headed away from us. We watched the progress of the moving vegetation, punctuated with a waving tail, reminiscent of the Cowardly Lion. And, we were so glad it was.

Cape Royal, North Rim of the Grand Canyon. In my wild and impetuous youth, a carload of us had gone out to watch the sunset. Heading home through the pitch black forest road, we rounded a hairpin turn to see a crouching figure in the middle of the road. We stopped just as the animal stood up—a large mountain lion. It was not in the least bit intimidated by our roaring engine or bright headlights. In fact, it was incensed. It drew back its lips in an angry hiss, tail churning the air like a cracking whip; the lion taming the humans. We all gasped. The puma spun around in one graceful motion and stomped off into the forest, tail waving grandly the whole time. When the cat drama queen slid into darkness on the other side, the entire car burst into exhales and exclamations.

One Samhain, sitting on the back patio with a small fire in the chiminea, we prepared for our ceremonial burning of lists of negativity we did not wish to bring with us into the dark time of the year. On that unusually warm October evening, we discussed our personal lists. Then, ready to toss them into the flames, the shriek of all shrieks shredded the night. Its echo hung in the air and slid down our necks, haunting us for hours after. Somewhere, a mountain lion had recited its list.

But the absolute best mountain lion story belongs to my friend, former colleague, and neighbor Allison Hays. Here is her story.

> She was a young seasonal ranger at Zion National Park. Her boyfriend had just asked her to marry him, a big decision for anyone. So, like many of us in times of intense emotion, she turned to nature to help sort things out and decide. She hiked into the backcountry planning her night vision quest. Setting up her camp back from a stream, she hiked to the water, inspired by its clarity. She settled onto a boulder watching the water, lost in thought. Several hours ticked by as she listened to water sluice over rocks, thinking. Coming back to the present, she realized it was getting dark. She turned to rise from the boulder only to encounter within arm's reach, a cougar. It pulled back its lips in a hiss, looking straight into Allison's eyes. She returned the stare, trying to show that she, too, had predator eyes. How long had it been creeping up on her as she remained lost in her own thoughts, water masking any

possible sound? It was a stalemate; someone had to make the first move. Allison thought if she could stand up quickly, it would then see her taller, and possibly threatening. She adjusted enough to get her legs under her, planning to spring upwards. In one swift move, the cougar spun around, brushing the length of its long ropey tail across Allison's face as it fled into the dusk.

These cats have more names than any other animal in this hemisphere, almost as many names as there are for a supreme deity. The word "cougar" is from the Tupis of the Amazon, meaning "predator the same color as the deer." The word "puma" comes to us from the Quechua of Peru, meaning "mighty magic animal." The Incas laid out the capitol city of their empire, Cusco, in the shape of a puma. In 1500, Amerigo Vespucci spied one on a beach in Central America. It's fitting that it was the first large animal he saw, as it was the widest ranging animal of the New World; from Chile to Canada. When the Spanish invaders encountered them they thought the cats were small, female African lions. So, since this cat lived mostly in the mountains, Europeans dubbed them "mountain lions." "Catamount" comes from a contraction of "cat of the mountains."

These cats are only limited by terrain that will provide them cover and food. Open spaces limit their specialty for surprise attack. When stalking prey, the hind paws fit neatly into the tracks already left by the front paws, those retractable claws never showing in footprints.

Dark markings around the eyes and lining the cheek to the nose strike a contrast to the white muzzle and chin—a beauty among cats. From nose to the burned-black tip of the ropey tail, males can be eleven feet long, weighing 145-200 pounds, females closer to 100. These cats have a small, flexible skeletal structure, but is mostly made up of muscle and sinew. Their three to five-inch paws with retractable one-inch claws hit its prey with all the delicacy of a floored diesel pickup truck. A crouching cat, with an intense, unbroken gaze, will flatten its ears against its head and twitch its tail to show it is ready to attack. Cats can jump 30 feet across from Point A to Point B, jump 18 feet straight up in the air on legs built like springs, and jump out of trees from 60 feet. In short spurts, pumas have been clocked at 45 mph. They have 30 muscles in their ears for swiveling, compared with 6 muscles in a human ear. Their night vision is six times stronger than human sight. Their gastronomical capacity is astounding—able to consume 18 pounds of meat in one sitting, preferably deer or elk calves. They drag away their prey and bury the leftovers under leaves and twigs, snacking on smaller animals in between larger meals. Cougars hate to fail—so once an attack has started, they will hang on with teeth, claws, and all that muscle.

The bone design in their throat makes it impossible for cougars to roar. But they can growl and hiss, and females call their cubs with an almost bird-like chirping. Chuffing, a small cough, is also a communication tool.

Mountain lions evolved into the perfect carnivorous predator. Unlike other top predators, cats will eat only meat. Modern cougars appeared around 300,000 years ago. When the giant saber-toothed cats disappeared, the cougars were ready to fill in the void.

Petroglyphs of mountain lions from 700 years ago show the Ancients' awe and reverence. The pictures tell of the fearsome weapons of the cat, particularly their teeth and claws, with that ropey tail in evidence. Early cultural names and beliefs surrounding the mountain lion reflect their respect for this creature: Cherokee—Lord of the Forest, and Cree—Greatest of Wild Hunters. Zuni believe cougars carry messages between the gods and people. Hopi revere the cat as a guardian kachina. Native Americans of many tribes performed ceremonies using the paws, teeth, hides, claws, and heads of pumas.

Cougars win the wildlife sexual marathon award—mating 50-70 times a day for a week, with the female being the temptress, which may be why "cougar" has come to mean a mature woman going after a younger man. Rrrrroooww. When the female cougar passes out of estrus, the relationship ends with the male going in search of another receptive female. But it is a tempestuous relationship, as mountain lion males have been known to later kill the female and her cubs.

Animal Damage Control was a federal program begun in 1931. Any animal with fangs and claws was deemed "injurious to agriculture." Over 66,000 cougars in 13 western states fell victim to aircraft, guns, poison, traps and state bounty systems. Slowly, and only in the remote, rugged landscapes of the West, the cougars started a comeback. Residing mainly west of the Mississippi, there are still occasional sightings in the east, and a small remnant population in Florida.

The growth in both human and mountain lion populations increases the chance of their paths crossing. In over 200 years of cougar records, statistics show that fully half of all attacks on humans have occurred between 1990 and now. But with only twelve fatal attacks on humans in North America during the 20th century, it's hard to justify the continued assault on cougars. For every 1200 people struck by lightning, there is one puma attack. Trophy hunters going for the big adult males wipe out the part of the cougar population least likely to attack. Unlike the multi-tasking females, big males are secure in their territory. The gangly juveniles out on their own for the first time, searching for territory, unsure of the rules, tend to be the ones just a tad too curious and get into trouble.

Mountain lions show up in odd places. A Prescott, Arizona, study in 2006 monitored 18 mountain lions, twelve of which regularly visited urban residential neighborhoods. One radio-collared male from the Black Hills in 2009 met his death in 2011 getting hit by an SUV in Connecticut, a distance of 1800 miles. In broad daylight in a Safeway parking lot in Lewiston, Idaho, a puma appeared in 2011. In 2012, a cougar tried entering Harrah's Casino in downtown Reno, but was flummoxed by the revolving door. Also in 2012, an Oregon couple awoke to find a mountain lion prowling their bedroom. Piecing the story together later when their heart rates slowed, they realized it had come through the doggie door chasing after their dog. The cat smartly remembered the way it got in and exited the same way.

Apparently, mountain lions love human children the way a domestic cat loves to bat at yarn. On a trail near Boulder, Colorado, a seven-year-old and his father held hands as they hiked to the parking lot when a female cougar pounced on the boy. Fortunately enough people armed with sticks and stones convinced her to let go. And a la *Life of Pi*, a 1930s account off the west coast of Vancouver Island had motorboat operator Jacob Armet spot a dog and turn toward it. But it was a mountain lion clambering aboard. Pulling up a seat to whack the cat, he unfortunately also struck the rudder. The next scene would have been fodder for a Keystone Cops routine if it weren't so harrowing. Ultimately Armet managed to get the boat under control and the cat back in the water with an extremely scratched boat to corroborate his tale.

The winner of the most bizarre cougar attack happened on Vancouver Island. The isolated cougar gene pool on Vancouver Island may include a genetic predisposition for aggressive behavior. The tight quarters on the island between predator, natural prey, and encroaching humans result in frequent encounters. Just like certain gangs are known for high crime, this population is the most dangerous gang in the mountain lion world.

In 1951 at a remote cabin on Vancouver Island, just as Ed McLean started to undress for bed, a cougar smashed through the plate glass window and attacked the man. He battled the cat toward the kitchen to grab a knife, stabbing the cougar enough that it let go. Wearing only his long underwear, he slammed the door between himself and the cat, listening to the wounded cat breathing heavily on the other side of the door, but leaving Ed outside on a cold January night. Six miles from the nearest neighbor, he rowed himself across a bay over rough water in stiff winds. Arriving exhausted, he found the door locked, but this almost super human broke into the house and phoned for help. Rescuers helped him, as well as returned to Ed's cabin to kill the cougar, which was curled up on the bed, bleeding profusely.

To coexist with these magnificent, top-of-the-food-chain predators, we need to give them uninterrupted space, tolerance, and respect. They are a true testament to the nature of pure wild.

X
Bobcat

There are no streetlights at the North Rim of the Grand Canyon. While driving my last shuttle run for the evening, I headed away from the Camper Store. The headlights picked up a crouching something in the road. Slamming on the brakes, I stopped just in time to see a bobcat caught in full glare. Looking up with annoyance, it blinked its big eyes. The headlights perfectly displayed the beauty of its tawny, greyish coat, spotted fur, short tail and perky ears. It feigned a lunge to the right, then turned and ran back into the forest. Though brief, it seemed a long gift of observation time for that encounter.

At our teacher apartment on the South Rim, a messy rainstorm created a mud bog in the backyard, splashing up onto the back porch. Unable to clean it up right away, I went out days later to work on the mess, and found a series of paw prints. Definitely too big for a domestic cat. I tried to match the prints using some animal books I had. To be sure, I took some pictures of the track and showed them to a biologist at the Science Center. "Bobcat," he said. "Definitely bobcat." Wow! On my back porch. The thought of having that elusive predator just outside my kitchen window was a thrill, one of the many perks of living inside a national park.

Survivor. Tough and scrappy. Master of elusiveness. The most common wildcat with sightings in all states except Delaware. Most bobcats prefer to stay within a range of only several acres, and since rabbits tend to congregate in about that space, they make a bobcat's work much easier. But, depending on the level of abundant food sources, bobcats may be pulled farther afield looking for tiny meals. They are highly adaptable and will eat something as big a fawn or as small as a bird, but their favorite dinner is jackrabbit. Large prizes need to be cached for a later meal, however rabbits or anything smaller can be devoured in one sitting. Just like human children, bobcats like to play with their food after it's dead and unlikely to get away. Keen eyes and ears are used to track their prey. Nocturnal, silent stalking leads to the capture of any unwary creatures. Hind paws go right into the same footprint as their front paws for added stealth, retractable claws leaving no trace.

Bobcats can jump twelve feet across, eight feet high, and run for up to 30 mph in short spurts. Usually they make a sudden lunge for their prey when they feel they are close enough to succeed. A bobcat goes from a soft, supple, low crouch to a springing, snarling mass of teeth and claws in a blur, biting at the neck. Raspy ridges on the roof of the mouth help to grind prey up on the way down. They are masters of precision hunting. They have to be; the prey doesn't stick around to give a bobcat a second chance.

The spotted fur on their torso contrasts strikingly with their striped legs, showing off that four to seven-inch bobbed tail. The tip of that tail is black on top and white underneath. The extra fur around their jowls is a distinguishing feature, looking like the muttonchops on Victorian era men in a sepia picture. Three times the size of a domestic cat, there's no mistaking them for your tabby. Black and white patterns on the back of the ears perhaps help the little ones to keep mama in sight. But, when those ears are twisted forward so that the white part shows, it is a sign of extreme agitation.

The bobcat first appeared in North America 600,000 years ago, descending from the Eurasian lynx and crossing via the Bering land bridge between Ice Ages. Since the bobcat is low on the ladder of predators, it has to work harder to safeguard its kill from being pilfered by something bigger. Perhaps that is what makes this animal an interesting combination of being both extremely aggressive and a patient watcher.

They inhabit any place that provides cover: canyons, forests, swamps, or broken woodlands. Temperate forest regions are their favorite habitat, not the wide open prairie. In the few areas where bobcat and lynx territories overlap, the scrappy bobcat doesn't hesitate to take on the much larger lynx. Bobcats are opportunists for denning, taking over any existing possible den, even sometimes appropriating an old beaver lodge. Solitary except for mating, each cat establishes and marks its own territory by scratching, urinating,

© Val Jesse

defecating or using its scent glands rubbed on bushes. Males and females don't live together, but are aware of each other's nearby territories. When it's time to mate, the female lets the male know by her not-so-subtle caterwauling. Kits, three to four per litter, stay with mama for a year, going from cute balls of fluff to proficient hunters and keen observers of their environment. When there is plentiful prey, a bobcat can live to be fifteen years old.

Bobcats have been targets for annihilation as pests and for their beautiful fur. But bobcats are actually a beneficial species, helping to keep the rodent populations under control. They rarely attack livestock. "Sport" hunting for trophy heads is something that even the ever feisty bobcat can't fight against. But bobcats have managed to survive and even thrive, never becoming an endangered species like so many others previously discussed in this book.

XI
Peregrine Falcon

That wide, sweeping curve that brings the rafts along the cliff wall on river-left makes Unkar Rapids one of my favorite on the Colorado River. By looking backwards just as the boat is entering the rapid, there is a quick-caught glimpse of Angel's Window high and far away on the North Rim. With secure handhold and feet braced, I twisted backwards, trying to sight that huge hole in the Kaibab limestone. What I saw instead was the brown and white speckled underfeathers of a peregrine falcon. Its steely gaze followed the boat as we whooped and hollered our way through the rapid. It stayed with us over the raft, swooping side to side, seemingly excited by our noisy progress. When we came off the white water into the calm, it dove a little closer to us then abruptly pulled up like a stunt pilot, soaring higher and higher, until it was just a moving speck along the distant Coconino Wall. It was as if we had an extra passenger enjoying the ride on currents of air.

When my husband Keith worked as a ranger at Phantom Ranch, we often strolled through the campground to appreciate the sounds of the sparkling Bright Angel Creek. Once as we walked by one of the picnic ramadas, I heard a noisy scratching and rustling sound. I slowly walked forward, leaned around the corner, and something leaned back at me from the rafters. Once my eyes adjusted to the shady darkness, I saw the blue-grey feathered back and intense gaze of a peregrine falcon. Huge eyes encircled in yellow were close enough for me to see the hooked beak, with yellow around the nostrils, the soft rust-colored breast with black speckles, and the formidable yellow talons. It spread its wings, revealing the striped feathers on the underside. I bowed under it, trying to get a closer look. The bird bowed back to me. I repeated the bow, and so did it. We slowly kept up this odd Japanese dance for more than a minute until the falcon, tiring of all this formal ritual, hopped farther down the rafter where it could fly out from under the shelter's roof away into the canyon.

The other birds don't stand a chance. The peregrine's favorite food is a bird in flight, and with its built-in 200 mph diving power, it's the fastest bird in the world. Flying level, they're fast enough, clocked at 100 mph. But it's the behavior called "stooping" that gets dinner. Starting on a high perch, such as a rocky cliff ledge or a window ledge of a skyscraper, they push the throttle forward into the sky up to heights of 1000 feet above the starting point. Then, they fold their wings and dive, a shrill sound of wind whistling through their feathers as they plunge. Specialized nostrils control airflow, helping them to breathe at those tremendous speeds. Even when they're not hunting, they still play in the air currents or gusts of wind. But, if those keen eyes spot prey on the fly, those huge talons are out, and they hit the hapless bird, sometimes snatching it out of the air and taking it off to the nestlings or stunning the bird and knocking it to the ground to be pounced upon and eaten.

Found on all continents except Antarctica, peregrine falcons have long been both admired and revered. The word "peregrine" comes to us from Latin, meaning "wanderer." Ancient Egyptians worshiped the falcon as the god Horus, meaning "that which is above." They believed falcons brought the sun to begin the new day and saw them as symbols of transformation, rebirth and eternal life. Falcons were mummified right along with notable humans. On this continent, the Cree refer to peregrines as mystic birds, bringing guidance from the Great Spirit. So this bird has been a witness to the rise and fall of many civilizations.

Prior to the invention of guns, falconry was the sport of nobles. Ancient Chinese and Persians established the art of falconry, with evidence of the sport in India and Sumer. Eggs or baby falcons were stolen from nests, and the chicks imprinted on their human captors, proving to be surprisingly docile and willing hunting assistants after training. Hoods, with a plume for quick removal, helped keep the birds calm by tricking, or "hoodwinking" them into believing it was nighttime. By the 1600s, falcons had lost their noble status and were seen more as pests and competition for food.

Their habitats became compromised as people hacked into the wilderness. But their populations remained relatively stable

worldwide until after World War II. Then, toxic chemicals began
to be widely used, and just as widely, peregrines began dramatically
disappearing. The entire eastern United States was suddenly absent
of breeding peregrines. It took a while for scientists to pinpoint the
cause—DDT. Because peregrines are at the top of their food chain,
the concentration of accumulated toxins from the seeds, plants,
insects, and birds full of DDT either killed the peregrines outright,
or produced eggs with almost translucent, fragile shells. Before the
falcons disappeared entirely, breeding programs were set up in 1964
in several countries, with releases back into the wild. Those captive-
bred baby birds were placed in a hack box where food was provided.
Eventually allowed to fly free, the bird returned to the box where
food was kept. Finally the box was closed, forcing the bird to rely on
instincts for hunting.

Truly adaptable, peregrines have thrived—some even choosing
to live in big cities due to the tasty, never-ending pigeon populations.
City-dwelling peregrines engender respect and gratitude among the
human onlookers, furthering the falcon's position as necessary to
ecological balance. But in places that still use pesticides the fate of

peregrines remains uncertain. Some subspecies of falcons migrate up to 9,000 miles because their food source does, bringing them into contact with lands still laced with toxic chemical soup.

An interesting story of the resilience of peregrines occurred during World War II. There was an all-out slaughter of peregrines along the British coast to protect the carrier pigeons returning with reports from the U-boat patrols. Fortunately, that population was able to rebound after the war ended.

Belonging to the larger group of birds of prey which includes hawks and eagles, peregrines are a raptor, meaning they are hunters who seize their meat by force. They are strikingly beautiful and regal in countenance. Yellow talons consist of three black curved toes in the front and one in the back, each knife-edge sharp. The female is the larger of the mated-for-life-pair, with a 45-inch wingspan swept back during flight and a 20-inch body. Their binocular-like eyes are huge for the bird's size—each weighing an ounce. Broad, dark stripes below each eye extend to the chin. That curved metallic-colored beak has a notch which serves as a tooth to kill in the air. Feathered pantaloons go all the way down to their claws. There are many near misses, for if the prey changes direction suddenly, the peregrine is going too fast to pull out of the dive. Sometimes the falcon stuns the prey, but loses its grasp. But that fast peregrine can swoop around and grab it again before it ever hits the ground. All these aerial acrobatics use a lot of energy, so a peregrine must eat about a quarter of its weight daily. The bird's "crop," or temporary storage pouch, protrudes from its chest after a big meal. They shove the leftovers into cracks in high ledge places for later. Their habitat needs to include water, as they bathe frequently.

They are creatures of habit, returning year after year to the same nesting site, or eyrie. Often generations continue to return. One particular eyrie in Australia has been scientifically dated back 19,000 years, and one in Wales has been continuously occupied since 1243 CE.

Peregrines stake out their territory, the males driving others away. Courtship begins in late winter or early spring by age three or four with established pairs renewing their vows. The male, called a tiercel, shows off with aerial displays, wooing the female to join in his soaring loops and dives. He may kill a bird to bring to the eyrie, hoping the female will follow. But she may have other ledges in mind. They eventually work it out, scraping a hollow for the three to four speckled eggs, ranging in color from cream to pink to ocher. During the 33-day incubation period, the male takes an occasional turn on the eggs, which are half the size of a chicken egg. Mostly the male provides food during this time. The chicks tend to sit on their bum, legs straight out ahead, a noisy fluff of down, so ugly as to be cute. With an abundant food source, peregrines can live up to 20 years. But large owls and golden eagles are a danger to the baby peregrines.

Rachel Carson sounded the alarm in 1962 with her book, *Silent Spring*. Organic farming, crop rotation, and plant diversity are how we humans survived as a species for eons. But modern man has introduced damaging practices that threaten that survival, most made in the name of dubious progress or questionable improvement. The conservation of water and soil is necessary since that is where the food chain starts, for us as well as the animals which share our planet. Do we really need more biological experiments on our fragile planet? Would we really want to live in a world that can't support the soaring wings of the peregrine falcon?

© ValJesse

XII
Condor

I had yet to see a condor. After the California condor reintroduction program began at Grand Canyon in 1996, my fellow residents documented many sightings. I spent most of my spare time outdoors, but so far, no condor. Disappointed, I stalked the rim looking for the giant birds. Talking with the Peregrine Fund people monitoring the condors, I asked what clues to look for. They described the giant, 9.5-foot wingspan, the white triangle on the underwing feathers, the red head, the giant beak. But, how can I pick them out from other birds flying over the canyon, I wanted to know. One of the researchers, in hushed tones, said "Oh, you will know."

And, she was right. Watching ravens squawk and cavort, or turkey vultures carving arcs in the sky, is nothing like the dark speck coming from the North Rim, wings straight out, no flapping. As it gets closer,wingtip feathers separate like fingers, except they're two feet long, the only thing moving to keep this bird on course. Nearing the rim, he turns his head slightly, legs and tail down. The crowd on the canyon's edge erupts into a spontaneous roar, awed by the sight of this almost extinct bird flying overhead. What a thrill to see it over the canyon, its ancestral range.

At the tip of Shoshone Point, my black Lab lay panting in the summer sun, perfectly still. Perhaps a little too still. An updraft brought a California condor level with the point. The whoosh of wings turned into a roar as it maneuvered into a landing position. My dog, startled by the enormous shadow suddenly hovering over her, abruptly sat up. With disappointment, the condor turned back to soar over the canyon. Live dogs aren't as interesting as dead ones for a member of the vulture family.

My sister-in-law had never been to Grand Canyon, and of course, we wanted to show it to her right. At Cedar Ridge she wanted to go all the way out to the point. We let her go to have her own experience with the canyon. Not only did she experience the canyon, but as she stood on the edge of the point, a California condor flew up out of the canyon right over her head. She threw her arms up in that universal symbol of joy as she watched it fly over her toward the cliffs.

At Grand Canyon Schools, recess duty could be interesting. Elk, deer, and numerous birds frequented the playground. But the show-stopper was a California condor nonchalantly landing on the roof of my library building. It sat there preening and peering about while I gathered students to give a very teachable moment about this rare bird. Of course, the Peregrine Fund was called and the students were ordered back inside. But for a few moments, those kids witnessed the results of one of the most intensive efforts in conservation sitting on their school roof.

My friend and best hiking buddy, Stacey, and I went to Plateau Point for a day hike. There's a place to scramble around some rocks for an extraordinary view. We scampered around in the rocks, and suddenly found ourselves within ten feet of a totally unconcerned condor. We gawked for a while, then went to look at the river. When we came back, the condor was in the same spot, thrilling other hikers, and preening; a cleansing movement made by running its feathers through its beak. It must have been the equivalent of the Saturday night bath for that condor.

But the most thrilling of all my condor encounters I witnessed alone. On some hot summer mornings I would rise with the sun and go to the Kaibab Trailhead and hike down to Skeleton Point. Usually the trails were empty or sparsely traveled by hikers at that time of day. I was down below O'Neill Butte when I came around a blind corner and found myself six feet away from a condor perched on a rock on the outside of the trail. This wasn't just any condor, with wingtags and radio transmitters attached. This condor, about six months old, had recently fledged and had not yet been captured for tagging. It was extremely nervous by my presence, so I backed away to give it all the room it needed. I stayed within visual range, and it kept looking at me. So I began to tell it how much it meant to all of us that it was a wild-born condor chick, free to fly in its rightful place over the Grand Canyon, and that we all were rooting for its survival. I told it that we were sorry some humans had made such a mess of its habitat and performed all that senseless slaughter. I said that not all people were like that; some of us revered its Pleistocene heritage and its right to be here. It cocked its head from side to side, looking at me now with curiosity rather than fright. I told it there is a dedicated group of scientists working hard to ensure its survival and the survival of its species. It flapped its wings a few times, and began to hop around on the rock. Enough of my speech. Fly, baby condor, fly!

And off it went, unfettered, stepping out and catching a thermal with the Grand Canyon as a backdrop, soaring over buttes and mesas, until it was just a speck on the horizon. I sat down on a rock and wept.

My husband, as a ranger, has his own condor encounter story. He tells it here.

My Condor

As an interpretive ranger on the South Rim of Grand Canyon National Park, I occasionally took groups of hikers down the South Kaibab Trail to Cedar Ridge. I had stops along the trail where I gave a short talk about geology, natural history, or human history of the area.

On one such hike, I had made my regular stop at Ooh-Aah Point, about .9 mile down the trail, a great viewpoint up and down the canyon. Some people coming up the trail said there was a California condor standing in the middle of the trail just a few switchbacks below Ooh-Aah. I wasn't in any hurry to confront a condor; so we waited until everybody was good and rested.

Sure enough, we came across a full-grown condor standing right in the middle of the trail. Some hikers had climbed up on the embankment beside the trail to get around it, but others were waiting for me, the ranger, to do something about this ugly, three-foot-tall bird with the big, dangerous beak.

Had this condor learned to beg? Those reintroducing condors to the wild were very worried about condor-

81

human interactions. If condors learned people would feed them, they would become dependent on them and never be the wild species they once were. The condor reintroduction program was only a year old, so I wasn't exactly sure what to do about this endangered species standing on the trail.

I got my Park Service radio out of my backpack and called Dispatch. I explained the situation. Dispatch asked me if I'd had hazing training. I supposed hazing training would be learning how to properly scare a condor off the trail.

I hadn't even heard of hazing training.

Eventually the dispatcher told me I had to have my group climb off the trail to get around the condor. So we did.

We continued about 100 yards down the trail when Dispatch called me back. It seems the dispatcher had gotten a hold of The Peregrine Fund people and they wanted me to scare the condor off the trail.

I returned to the condor. It had watched this whole interchange quite bemusedly.

I had two walking sticks which I waved in the air while yelling as loud as I could. The condor must have felt threatened because it started flapping its wings until it was hovering at a level close to my face. I jumped back a few feet. The condor landed on a large rock lining the outside of the trail.

I advanced yelling and hitting my walking sticks on the ground behind the bird. It took a little time, but eventually the huge bird spread its giant wings and stepped off the rock into the space over the edge of the trail. The terrain dropped quickly then stretched outward to the edge of oblivion way down below.

The condor swooped down, cleared the cliff and floated out into the wildness that is the Grand Canyon.

On a side note, as our tour group was hiking in the Peruvian Andes, a fellow hiker and I took a different path than the rest of the group. And I am so glad we did, because we were the only ones who got to see a fly-by of an Andean condor, slightly larger cousin to the California condor.

Condors are virtually unchanged from the time when they were contemporaries with the saber-tooth tiger and mastodon about ten million years ago. Ancient condor bones have been found in such

diverse habitats as Florida, the Rocky Mountains, upstate New York and the Pacific coast. They evolved in the Pleistocene, dining on creatures the size of a woolly mammoth—ten tons and fourteen feet high, so condors had to be big.

Revered and immortalized in petroglyphs, Native Americans called them thunderbirds. Ceremonial dancers put on the wings and skin of a condor like a cloak. Sometimes condor bones were included in burial sites or made into whistles. Feathers were used for adornment and ceremonies. Solstice windows were designed to throw streaks of sunlight onto paintings of the thunderbird. Some tribes believed condors controlled the weather. Some Native traditions say condors hatched the human race.

Lewis and Clark both noted in 1806 that this was the largest bird they had seen in North America; and they took time to sketch a detailed drawing of the great bird's head.

Telescopic eyes with six to eight times better vision than humans, beak knife-edge sharp, this bird is finely tuned as a scavenger to find carcasses and rip into them. That common predator habit of dragging prey away and covering it with dirt and leaves may come from an attempt to hide the carcasses from the sharp-eyed condor.

Condors weigh in at an astronomical 25 pounds—a heavy-weight champion in the avian world. The only sound they make besides audible breathing is a hissing noise. On flat ground with a belly full of meat they are very awkward, needing a running start to become airborne. According to reports by some helicopter pilots, condors can fly as high as 10,000 feet, gliding effortlessly on straight, outstretched wings with miles between flaps, at 50 mph. Their crop, an expandable neck pouch to carry food, can hold up to three pounds of meat, handy for regurgitating to their young. The condor has no sense of smell, luckily, as it does have some rather disgusting habits, such as sticking its head into dead creatures to get at those grisly, gory morsels. It also urinates on its own feet as part of its body's cooling system, called urohydration. It has an ugly, wrinkled, red head naked of feathers since it spends so much time in bloody carcasses.

After the ancient megafauna became extinct, many scavengers died out. But one remained. Condors managed to adapt, but dwindled. Humans crossing from the Bering Strait didn't take kindly to condors trying to hone in on their hard-won kills, which included dead whales. And so began the conflict between humans and condors. Later, habitat destruction, toxic chemicals and wanton shooting reduced the population. There was also a huge number of "scientific" collectors who shot and stuffed birds for "studying."

An egg collecting craze in the late 1800s also helped to decimate the condor numbers. Because they can live up to 45 years, they have a very slow reproduction rate. A mated pair produces one pale, bluish green egg every other year. Eagles are a predator of the young condors, while ravens try to eat the eggs.

But the real assassin is lead poisoning from lead bullets ingested when condors eat from uncollected hunting carcasses or carelessly left gut piles full of lead shot. The wild condor population was reduced to a straggling group in southern California, extirpated in all of their previous ranges. Scientists, in a last ditch effort to save the species, made the extremely difficult and highly controversial decision to capture all remaining 27 condors and bring them in for a captive breeding program. The last wild and free condor was captured on April 19, 1987. The photograph of that capture is heart wrenching, grim-faced scientist pinning the bird to the ground. Some think it was the darkest hour in American conservation.

It has not been easy, but the condor recovery program is working. Thirty years later, the captive breeding program has been successful to the point of allowing releases back into the wilderness.

Debate was heated and plentiful about where to release them. It had to be a protected place, huge, within their historic range, remote, with limited human intrusion, somewhere with cliffs, ledges, caves, water, strong updrafts, and a steady population of large mammals. Grand Canyon National Park certainly fit the bill, errr, beak.

Each bird has a tag number on the shoulder and under the wing, and a radio transmitter which is constantly monitored by radio telemetry. The condors are recaptured regularly to check for lead poisoning and to begin chelation therapy if necessary. California, Grand Canyon and Baja California now have active populations, with the breeding programs continuing as well.

Fall, 1996. 700 people gathered at the base of the Vermilion Cliffs in the remote Arizona strip, the release site for the California condors. All faces turned upwards to watch the birds soar, the condors turning instinctively toward the Grand Canyon.

It's been a challenge with so many of the released birds having no mentor/parent birds to guide them through their awkward juvenile years. The puppet-reared captive babies just weren't getting the memo on how to survive in the wild. Young condors gathered on people's decks. On the Hualapai Reservation, a condor hung around the airstrip and eventually ended up in the pilot's lounge. The door was locked, and biologists were called, but it took a while for them to arrive. When the door was eventually opened, there sat the condor on a chair, calmly watching the NBC coverage of the war in Kosovo, amidst the completely trashed mess made by the condor.

Because "friendly" condors were most at risk, Peregrine Fund workers were trained in hazing the birds to leave human inhabited areas, particularly on the South Rim. There crowds gather to gawk at the canyon and condors, and condors gather to gawk at the tourists, hoping at least one of them is dead.

Hunters who insist on using lead ammunition instead of the less fragmenting copper bullets are all that stand between the success and failure of the California Condor Recovery Program. The condor's struggle to survive in the wild is directly linked to our efforts to preserve wilderness.

The more removed from humans, the better for the condors. They are allergic to human's toxic chemicals, habitat destruction, trash which they mistake as food, and guns.

We are their only predator.

XIII
Golden Eagle

It was our early morning commute from Flagstaff to Tuba City. Cresting the hill on Highway 89, we began the long downhill run with the sweeping vistas of the Navajo Reservation, "the Rez", to locals. It was my day as a passenger, so I watched the scenery. Suddenly, a dark object hurtled toward the car from the left. A golden eagle flapped frantically, jackrabbit dangling from its talons, trying to get airborne with its breakfast. The eagle cleared the car, but the jackrabbit grazed the windshield, leaving a smear of blood. Finally airborne, the eagle continued its flight toward the rising sun. Not often is the underside of an eagle seen that close up.

Out visiting friends on Woodland Ranch Road off Highway 64, I slowed the car, curious about a roadside commotion. Something was bouncing with an erratic rhythm. It was a golden eagle, jumping, wings outspread, footwork like a cocky prize fighter entering the ring. Then it changed its stance, wings curled in a protective semi-circle. It was trying to finish off a lively rabbit, and was now ready to eat its prize. But, here was I, a gawking distraction. The eagle gave me an amber-eyed, dismissive look, beak parted slightly, panting from the exertion. I meekly departed, moving the car down the road, leaving the predator to enjoy its hard-earned repast.

Eagles are found on every continent except Antarctica, living mostly in the northern tiers. In North America, the bald eagle is most closely related to the European vultures, while the golden eagle's closest relative is the red-tailed hawk. The golden gets its name from the light caramel colored feathers on its head and neck.

Ancient civilizations revered golden eagles, as evidenced by cave paintings. Babylonians and Syrians revered them as gods, while the Greeks believed eagles to be the messengers of Zeus. Romans created coins with eagle images. Eagle feathers are part of modern Highland funeral rites in Scotland. In present-day Mongolia, indigenous people train eagles to hunt red fox as a form of falconry.

Representing victory and pride, Native Americans have long honored the golden eagle as the Sun god or Sky god. Early Native Americans ambushed golden eagles, grabbing the bird's legs and plucking out feathers. This act of bravery was supposed to put the captor in touch with the Great Spirit. Some tribes now have special use permits to keep golden eagles in order to gather the feathers. The feathers are still used in headdresses or fans.

With a seven to eight-foot wingspan and a body length of forty inches, the female can weigh fourteen pounds, males up to a third smaller. They mate for life at around age five, returning to the same nesting area every year. They keep adding sticks to the nests, which become behemoths, sometimes crushing the tree branches and crashing to the ground. Therefore, eagles prefer cliff ledges to build their eyries for nesting to avoid such catastrophes. Sometimes several nests will be constructed in the same area to establish territory. Eagle eggs are about the same size as goose eggs, but more rounded. Creamy white with ocher dots, two to three eggs are laid several days apart. Sibling rivalry is fierce. When food sources are sparse, the eldest eaglet sometimes bullies the others, pushing them away from the food. Oddly, the parents do not interfere, and the youngest born seldom survives. But, when food is plentiful, all three may survive. The male brings the food, and the female tears it into tiny pieces to feed to the young. Fledging occurs in ten to twelve weeks, but parental feeding continues until the fall migration.

Their favorite meal is rabbit, a one-pound meal devoured in one sitting. They will eat carrion, often dive bombing other birds and bullying them away for the choicest feeding spots. They regurgitate pellets of the indigestible parts of prey—great for scientists to study exactly what the eagles are eating. Goldens will sometimes attack a solitary condor or go after a chick, but they quickly learn their lesson if there is more than one adult condor on a carcass. Conversely, gangs of ravens delight in picking on a lone eagle in flight, but skedaddle when the mate appears.

Goldens love surveying their territory from snags. A golden eagle can spot a mouse from a mile away and can watch a rabbit from two miles. Those front-positioned eyes see eight times better than a human's. Their hearing is also acute, while their smell is almost non-existent. Talons are yellow and strong, with scythe-like claws. The steely grey curved beak with that sharp hook is highlighted by yellow around the nostrils and jawline, which makes the bird look like it is smiling. Pantaloons of feathers cover the legs. The eagle soars on thermal air currents around hills and mountains, keeping high aloft on long reconnaissance missions. Once it spots prey, it folds the broad wings and dives at speeds up to 180 mph, talons ready to grasp the prey when close. Tail feathers spread wide to steer and act as a brake.

In the wild, most eagles only survive to about 20 years. But in captivity, these great birds have survived up to 50 years. Once common across the western United States, and occasionally spotted as far east as North Carolina and Tennessee, golden eagle populations

plummeted during the 1900s. Habitat destruction was definitely part of the problem, but once again, the real culprit was DDT. Similar to the tragedy which affected peregrines, goldens suffered because they are the top predator of their food chain, belted with the accumulation of toxins, causing fragile, thin-shelled eggs. Deliberate poisoning, trapping, shooting, run-ins with electrical power lines, and being hit by cars are other human-caused hazards. Eagles have also been known to eat lamb carcasses, exposing them to the highly toxic sheep dip chemical, dieldrin, which has the same effect as DDT.

This magnificent top-tier predator continues to exist as a symbol of authority and strength. But, more than just a symbol, it plays a crucial role in helping with both rodent control and carcass clean-up. Eagles deserve wild lands free of human interference so they can continue to benefit our environment.

XIV
Ringtail

In the private dining room of the historic El Tovar Hotel we had our own waitstaff for our special celebration. Amid the clinking of real silver on plates with Mimbres designs and the delicate chime of crystal glasses, another sound emerged. It was the soft scratching of claws navigating the narrow space between the decorative ledge and the ceiling. Suddenly, peering down at us with great interest in our dinner of stuffed salmon was a ringtail. It perused the room, gathering all gazes in its direction. As if on cue, we all gasped and cooed. Then we were treated to a grand swish of its raccoon-like tail as it scurried to a small hole in the ceiling and disappeared.

During a river trip along the Colorado River, we camped at Zoroaster the night before hiking out. I sat, butt in the tent, legs stretched outside in the sand, separating out the items going up the trail with me and those continuing on down river. Darkness stole over camp while I was concentrating on my task. Hearing a commotion in the camp kitchen, I looked up and suddenly saw a creature appear between my sprawled legs. It sat up, head bent to one side, eyes shining brightly, looking at me with curiosity. It took a moment for me to register that there was a ringtail posed between my legs. I squealed in delight, and it leaped up with a flurry of fluffy tail and disappeared along the river bank.

My husband Keith worked at Phantom Ranch for 11 years. Here's his report about ringtails at the Ranch.

> Ringtails seem to enjoy living at the bottom of the Grand Canyon. These cute but pesky animals moved through the cracks in the rock walls of Phantom Ranch by slipping into the spaces around pipes in the ceiling. Many nights after the employees working Beer Hall locked up, the ringtails came down for a snack. Using their tails for balance, they managed to drop onto the

stove and then to the kitchen floor, eventually making it to the canteen window where food was sold. The candy stored under the window was popular with ringtails, which, oddly enough, ate only the Almond Joys, never Snickers, Pay Day, or Peanut Butter cups.

One night in the late 1970s, some of the Phantom crew were relaxing with a few beers in the back room of the lodge when Dave T., an avid fisherman, got the idea of "fishing" for ringtails. Tying a piece of twine to an Almond Joy, he then cast the line as far as he could into the attic and "trolled" for a bite. Dave repeated this process several times without success. Then he threw the Almond Joy out into the attic as far as he could and began to pull it back. That time, we heard a pounce and scratching sounds on top of the ceiling overhead.

"I got a bite," Dave yelled as the string drew tight.

Dave pulled harder. The string suddenly came loose, and there was another pounce tightening the string again. Eventually the action was within a foot of the hole. Dave gave a tug, and a half-eaten Almond Joy fell out of the hole. Behind it came the face of a ringtail with those big eyes looking at us all, trying to figure out what we were doing.

Visitors to the Phantom Ranch dining hall were occasionally treated to an appearance of a ringtail. There was a hole in the wall about three feet up, caused by an exuberant dancer at a staff party. Ringtails would pop their heads through the hole, delighting guests.

Around 3:30 a.m. I came into the lodge to be the morning waiter. This was summertime in the desert, so I automatically switched on the swamp cooler in the back room. The cooler made a loud banging noise and a cloud of dust and fur flew out of the cooler register. I immediately shut-off the cooler, and sad moans came from inside. I knew then that a ringtail had somehow crawled into the cooler. It must have had a horrible ride around and around when that cooler fan came on. Taking that cooler apart to see what was left of the ringtail was more than I could do alone. Besides, I had to serve breakfast to 44 hikers early enough so they could hike out of the Grand Canyon before it got too hot. I put a piece of tape across the cooler switch and went to work.

The back room is the employees' dining room; when the first employees came in to have breakfast, I told them the sad story. They immediately went to work disassembling the cooler. When they got the back panel off, a badly beaten ringtail hopped out. Although both of its back legs seemed broken, that ringtail used its front legs to pull itself up the rock wall of the lodge and made his escape.

We saw that ringtail many times in the next few years. It had regained the use of one of its hind legs but still had to drag the other leg behind it.

In the raccoon family along with the coatimundi, ringtails look like they've been constructed at an animal spare parts store. They have the comportment of a cat, a body like a weasel, a tail like a raccoon, the two-inch ears and face of a fox, and the acrobatic climbing ability of a squirrel. Their impressive tail is 16 inches long, with alternating black and white rings, ending with a black tip. The body is 15 inches long, but the creature is mostly furry fluff, weighing only two to three pounds. Short legs support this long body and tail arrangement. The huge, dark eyes are surrounded by a white ring to help in their nocturnal life. The body fur is yellowish grey, ends tipped in black, with the belly white. Its sharp retractable claws never show in the tracks of its five long toes. The hind feet can rotate 180° so the animal can jump and then run down trees face first. Like a flying squirrel, ringtails can leap across great distances.

Ringtails are an Arizona original, although their range extends throughout the Four Corners region, into northern and Baja Mexico and also the western tip of Texas. Ringtails inhabit the deserts and canyonlands. They are found at elevations up to 9000 feet, but prefer the upper and lower Sonoran zones. They "weasel" their way easily along high ledges, favoring rocky crevices, hollow trees, or shallow caves, sometimes residing in underground dens or even abandoned buildings. Cliffs and rocky canyons in the oak belt are favored habitats, but they will sometimes move to brushy arroyos in the desert for wintering.

Not at all picky omnivores, they are very fond of cactus fruit, and also dine on fish, reptiles, amphibians, birds, eggs, sweet berries, nuts, and insects. They are a small but mighty predator of mice, pack rats, and squirrels. They pounce on prey and dispatch it with a clean bite to the neck, gulping their victim down headfirst.

Usually a quiet, stealthy creature, a ringtail can bark, growl, or snarl if threatened. Ringtails mark their territory with urine and scat placed neatly in one big pile.

Mating occurs between February and June, with the female only in heat for three to six days during this time. The fuzzy, blind young are born about 65 days later in litters of one to five, leaving the den at around eight weeks old. They can live from six to nine years.

Historically, miners captured baby ringtails and kept them in the mines to aid in pest control, where the ringtails happily ate all the rodents, spiders, and scorpions. It's easy to see why the lonely miners of old adopted these adorable and curious creatures. They were both useful and amusing companions.

XV
Snake

During one of the Park Service's attempts at fire management, a team of firefighters wielding chainsaws showed up in my backyard on the South Rim. There was a standout of a snag behind the teachers' townhouses, a gnarled juniper stripped down to bare wood and partial branches. Raising its limbs skyward earned it the nickname "The Goddess Tree" because of its beseeching arms. When a young, attractive teacher realized we weren't home, she dashed out clad in her bikini and confronted the worker and his chainsaw. Startled, he listened to her lecture on habitat trees, and, perhaps dazzled by her outfit, allowed the tree to remain.

My dog Keetna started her funny yipping and dancing that for her could only indicate the presence of a snake. I went to the yard to investigate, but no snake. I realized the dog's gaze was higher than the ground, and looked toward the upper limbs of the gnarled snag of the spared juniper tree and gasped. There was a gopher snake climbing right up the tree like a cobra out of a snake charmer's basket, slithering into one hole and out another, reminiscent of that childhood circle game of "go in and out the window." It was gorgeous—yellow with brown markings, perhaps four feet long. It zigged and zagged its way around the outside of the trunk before disappearing inside. I saw it go at least twelve feet up, then slither back down to the ground. Birds had nested there previously that summer, and I wondered if it sensed the feathery nest. But it was too late for that egg sandwich, as those baby birds had already flown the coop. Spending time with a gopher snake moves one back in time to a primal state.

On a hike in remote Goblin State Park in Utah, we walked cautiously along a knife-edge ridgeline. A nervous gopher snake encountered our dog, rose high into the air with just the tip of its rattleless tail for balance on the earth. Our "scared-y" dog did her funny snake dance and yipped that "Mom, there's a snake" bark, performed a few feints and lunges in the snake's direction before scampering as far away as she could on that narrow trail. We waited until the snake composed itself and returned to the ground before attempting to squeeze past it on that exposed trail.

I wended my way up the steep South Kaibab Trail, panting, eyes glued to the rocky trail just before me. As the trail went ever upwards, I suddenly froze. Within six feet of me smack in the middle of the trail was the fattest Western diamondback rattlesnake I had ever seen. It was coiled, but I knew if it changed its mind, I was within striking distance. Somehow I managed to back up without tripping or falling. I must have vibrated the trail, because the snake shifted its position, tongue flickering in and out to identify me. "Sweaty human," it thought to itself.

Feeling a bit more comfortable now that there was some space between us, I was still faced with quite a dilemma. The trail was straight up to the left, navigable only to bighorns, and to the right a sheer dropoff. I needed the trail.

How does one gently encourage a fat, six foot, venomous snake to move? I tossed pebbles to the left of the snake, hoping to make it uncomfortable enough to move to the right. I continued a shaky barrage of deliberately misaimed stones, never intending to hit the creature. To my immense relief, it s-l-o-w-l-y uncoiled and made a lazy slither to the right. I waited until I saw that rattle disappear over the edge, then cautiously stepped forward. It was only about six feet below the trail, but that was enough for me.

It was the only time I ever sprinted uphill on the Kaibab Trail.

Keith, during his years as a ranger, told many stories of legendary creatures of the canyon.

I could mention such creatures as stick lizards, hoop snakes, and rattlecats. These stories probably explain why biologists never believed the accounts of pink rattlesnakes.

The story told at Phantom Ranch was that sometime in the 1960s, a team of biologists staying at the ranch doing some kind of survey fell into an argument about pink rattlesnakes with Mel, the Phantom Ranch manager. Mel did not have much education, so when he maintained he had seen them, the biologists told him that what he had actually seen was a regular western diamondback rattlesnake covered with pink dust from the canyon.

The next morning the team of biologists were eating breakfast when the dining room screen door flew open. Mel walked in with a live, pink rattlesnake in one hand and a bucket in the other. The biologists rather suddenly scraped their chairs back against the wall and watched. Mel had quite a time getting the tail of that coiling snake under his foot, so he stepped on it and stretched the snake out from head to tail. Finally he reached into the bucket of soapy water and with a stiff brush, scrubbed that poor rattlesnake from head to tail to the horror of the biologists. Then he held the still-squirming pink rattlesnake in front of the biologists' faces and pronounced, "See, it's still pink." I don't think there has been any question since that there is a separate sub-species of pink rattlesnakes found only in the Grand Canyon.

Reptiles are predators, and none more feared, yet venerated, than the snake. Only a fifth of the approximately 2,700 species of snakes are poisonous, but they're the ones that get all the press. A theory is that snakes started off as lizards, but evolved to live underground, dispensing with the need for limbs.

Snakes have represented an array of feelings from revulsion to reverence, death to life, evil to good, the highest wisdom and the basest desires. Cultures around the globe regard snakes in their mythology as possessing magical powers. Shown biting its tail in a never ceasing circle of life, the snake often shows up as a symbol for regeneration or rebirth. With snakes observed burrowing in the ground and re-emerging, they were also seen as messengers of knowledge from Mother Earth. Many cultures have elevated snakes to the level of a deity.

During molting, the snakeskin turns dark, the eyes become opaque, and the snake stops eating, mimicking a "little death." It's obvious from where the symbolism of regeneration springs when one sees a shiny new snake wriggle free and emerge from the old, discarded skin.

The importance of coloration as a method of survival cannot be overstated. Camouflage is the best weapon for snakes in all of their myriad ecozones. They really just want to be left alone. The splotches, bars, and stripes in complex, bead-like patterning blend in well with the rocky, sandy desert environment for our Southwestern snakes.

A snake's eyesight is actually poor, and its hearing is not anything we would recognize. That stereotypical snake charmer can throw away the flute—the snake is focusing on the player's movements and vibrations, not the sound. With no external ear appendages, snakes pick up on vibrations transmitted through the ground, using the lungs to help conduct the message along the length of the body to the brain.

With their body temperature being controlled by the environment, it is a constant battle for them to maintain temperature. Mornings bring snakes slowly from their burrows. They are unable to make rapid movements until basking in the sun for a morning warm-up, utilizing warm rocks to create radiant heating. Blood vessels on the surface of the skin dilate and send warmth down the length of the body. But when there is the need to retreat to shade to prevent over-heating, blood vessels reverse the process to move blood away from the skin to conserve heat as nighttime coolness moves in. The advantages of this system is that reptiles have a far broader temperature tolerance than other species. Therefore, they need much less food to keep their systems going. As a result, they can inhabit ecosystems too extreme for most birds and mammals, such as deserts. Their much slower breathing rate prevents water loss, which desert snakes mostly derive from their prey.

Since the whole body of the snake is always in touch with ground or rocks, any vibration of an intruder is noted and reacted to. Rattlesnakes have an additional advance warning system. Infrared radiation sensors called "pits" located between the eyes and the nostrils help detect temperature differences in the air, say, if a small trembling rodent is nearby. This is a handy system for helping hunt in total darkness. That eerie, flickering, forked tongue is actually testing for airborne scent particles, sensing if there could be prey nearby. These scents are then transferred to the Jacobson's organ, a specialized area on the roof of the mouth which transmits information to the brain via an olfactory nerve.

Their jaws have the ability to dislocate, enabling all snakes to swallow prey much larger than themselves. The teeth are pointed backwards to assist in swallowing the prey whole, headfirst.

Repeated contractions move the prey farther and farther into the snake's body. Extra saliva helps to slide the prey deeper. The snake slithers off to a hiding place for the arduous digestion process, which depending on the size of the prey, could take weeks. Once the bulge disappears, the snake is ready to be actively on the hunt again. Because snakes don't need to eat often, they can wait a long time between meals.

Rattle tail up, body in a coil, head raised, tongue flickering wildly—that diamondback rattlesnake is ready to strike. Its rattling tail is your final warning to back off; it has lightning reflexes when it does zero in on its prey. The fangs normally tucked into the roof of the mouth on hinges act as hypodermic needles to deliver the venom. The hollow fangs press on the reservoir of the deadly dose of poison, injecting it into its hapless victim. Rattlesnakes usually bite and then release the victim to stagger off, knowing it won't get far, and then follow at leisure when the prey is dead. Mature rattlesnakes control the amount of venom depending on the size of the victim. The venom includes neurotoxins which interfere with nerve impulses to the muscles, while cardiotoxins cause cardiovascular depression, including anaphylactic shock. Rattlesnakes are in the top three of the deadliest snakes in the world.

Gopher snakes mimic rattlesnake movements, coiling and raising up and "rattling" a rattleless tail, flattening its head into a triangular shape, hoping to fool anything threatening into thinking it is a rattlesnake. Gopher snakes actually kill by constriction.

Rattlesnakes engage in ritualized mating combat, complete with frontal raised body charging, followed by a writhing intertwining. Snakes tend to stick out their tongues and rub bodies during mating. Snakes have two methods of birth. Rattlers are ovoviviparous, (meaning live birth,) which lay "eggs" that are no more than a transparent membrane. Because the embryos are already highly developed, they break through the membrane easily. Gopher snakes are oviparous, producing actual eggs, which hatch after a short incubation. Most mother snakes coil around the eggs and emerging babies for protection for the first few days. After that, the young are on their own.

Habitat reduction, human-caused annihilation, and a trade in snake skins reduces local populations. But scientists are just at the beginning of learning about snake venom and its potential uses in pharmacology to aid humans. Snakes should be respected for being grand exterminators of rodent populations.

Snakes are so foreign, so completely different from anything else on land, in trees, or in water that they might have hailed from another planet. When one slithers into view, it almost always is a surprise. Camouflaged spectacularly to whichever environment it finds itself in, the snake often disappears right as our eyes finally focus on it.

XVI
Toad

Toad love. Right there on that fluid line dividing sand from the Colorado River. We spotted a pair of mounted toads while trotting back and forth with food, tables, and the trappings that 25 humans need for a wilderness lunch.

The plump female toad rested on the cool, damp sand while the smaller, but equally plump male mounted her and grasped her huge "love handles" with his tiny toad fingers. Completely ignoring us, they changed their location following only the movement of the river. They seemed completely unfazed by the endless traipsing of humans back and forth to the boats. No violent thrustings or screamings, just those Buddha-like, all-knowing smiles. Maybe this is what we all need more of—just sexy cuddling in nature.

What is a frog and what is a toad? Scientists don't discriminate —all are called anurans. Frogs are generally damp, with permeable, smooth skin, while toads are dry and warty. Long limbs for both equate with leaping, while shorter limbs are for walking or hopping. Those bulging eyes with the horizontal pupils and that wide-mouth grin make these amphibians project a genial nature.

Toads don't live in water, but do need to live near water in order to reproduce as their eggs lack a protective shell. Wherever their habitat, camouflage is a toad's best defense. So desert toads tend to be brown, grey, and spotted. Some species prevent drying out in the scorching desert summers by burrowing deep into the mud and emerging only when there is adequate rain, a process called "aestivating." Some burrowers have extra foot "blades" to help move the dirt. They dig and whip the dirt away, disappearing backwards into their holes for protection until the next rains arrive.

Respiration is a unique three-part system. Gills for the tadpoles, harkening back to their fishy ancestors. Unlike human bellow-like lungs, a toad's floor of its mouth raises and lowers for respiration.

Adults use their lungs as well as their skin to absorb moisture, since toads do not drink. Species living in the deserts are susceptible to water loss, and so use their lungs more, thus retaining valuable moisture through a thicker skin. When toads shed their skin, they eat it. Toads can lose almost half of their body weight in moisture during the dry spells and still survive.

Since they are cold-blooded, they must rely on the outside environment to activate their body systems. Around 70° is when they become active; 85° begins to get a tad warm for them. So they seek shade, go in water or burrow into the mud. 70-80° is their happiest temperature zone, which is why most live in the tropics. Even tadpoles like to hang out in the shallower part of their pool where the water is warmer. But toads can adjust—hibernating in winter or aestivating in summer.

Toads are carnivorous. What they eat is regulated by size, as they must swallow their prey whole because they have no teeth. That huge grinning mouth is for devouring large prey. So insects, ants, termites, spiders, slugs, snails, smaller members of their own species and aquatic larvae are all on the menu. Tadpoles have a more limited diet of algae or bacteria. Sometimes lying in wait, camouflaged, then springing up as an attractive meal saunters by is a good hunting technique. That long sticky tongue is lightning fast and highly accurate. It shoots out from the front of the mouth, catches an unwary insect, then retracts. Other toads root around in moss or leaf litter in order to pick off a marching row of ants one by one. Some toads burrow right into an ant or termite hill for easy pickings. Those bulging eyes aren't just cute—they're weapons for the hunt. Mucus glands which help to keep the skin moist also contain toxins as a defense for some species, such as the Colorado River toad. When confronted with a predator, a milky substance oozes forth, and one taste usually stops the attacker.

Toads are mainly nocturnal, except during breeding season. The smaller male toad clambering up onto the back of the much larger female and holding on behind her front limbs to mate is called "axillary amplexus." A few hours of amplexus is average, with some couples staying in that position for days or even a week. Their fertilized eggs are in long strings with a jelly-like cushioning, which are deliberately entangled in water plants. The eggs become larvae, which turn into swimming tadpoles, which grow legs, lose their tails, and crawl up to begin their lives on land. This life span takes advantage of ephemeral monsoon pools where no predators live.

The toad faces many environmental challenges. It is crucial for their lifecycle to have unpolluted water and appropriate land habitat to thrive on after their water stage, since they tend to inhabit the same general area year after year. They migrate locally in search of mates, food, and shelter, navigating by a combination of memory and sounding calls. Land razed for development, logging or agriculture denigrates their habitat. Limited geographic range leads to limited chances for survival. Agriculture, especially, causes chemical pollution. Domestic animals such as cats and dogs, and even rats are causing certain species of toads to go extinct. Fungal infections have also exacted a toll, perhaps because toads are already so stressed. The pet trade and road squashing cause many species to wink out.

The red-spotted toad that I saw along the Colorado River is able to flatten its three-inch body to squeeze into tiny crevices for escape. Toads can climb steep canyon walls in rough, rocky regions. Some species will inflate their bodies, looking more imposing to a predator. But immobility and camouflage remain their best defenses.

Their hearing is acute, as anyone who has ever heard an amphibian chorus can attest. Toads make their nocturnal location known by trills, croaks, chirps, grunts, whistles, and bellows. The tympanum, or eardrum, is hidden in a skinfold right behind the eye. Interestingly, the male's is always bigger. For the production of that mating call, the toad fills its lungs, closes nostrils and mouth, then forces air over the vocal chords and into the balloon-like vocal pouch.

The word amphibians comes to us from the Greek, "amphi" meaning "both" and "bios" meaning "life" referring to their need for both water and land to complete their life cycle. The earliest known fossils of amphibians were found in Greenland, and were over a yard long. Modern amphibians appeared about 200 million years ago, evolving from a fish called lobe-fins during the Devonian era.

Originally from fresh water lakes, these "fish" had to rapidly react and adapt to the sudden paucity of water.

Its engaging looks with bulging eyes and lazy smile made toads an easy target for anthropomorphism. References in mythology to frogs and toads go all the way back to the Egyptians, Chinese and East Indians. Native Americans revere the toad for its astonishing metamorphosis from egg to larvae to tadpole to adult toad. It disappears into Mother Earth and reappears with the rains, and has an amazing repertoire of sounds.

For some unknown reason, toads in Europe became more associated with the dark arts during the Middle Ages. From this darkness originates the fairy tale of a witch turning a handsome prince into a toad released only by the kiss of a beautiful maiden.

Personally, I know I had to kiss a lot of toads before I found my handsome prince.

XVII
Scorpion

I am fortunate because I have seen many a scorpion in my years at Grand Canyon, but I've never been stung. Scorpions are such iconic canyon denizens, and people always ask about them, so I've included my husband Keith's stories here.

There are millions of scorpions at the bottom of Grand Canyon. A favorite ploy of the rangers at Phantom Ranch is to take visitors out for a Scorpion Hunt at night with a black light. When exposed to ultraviolet light, scorpions glow, so every scorpion within range of that black light emits an eerie bluish light. The rocks and cacti seem to be crawling with scorpions. Some people can't sleep after that experience thinking they felt scorpions crawling on them. However, the incidence of visitors getting stung by scorpions near Phantom Ranch is fairly low. The most common cause of scorpion stings is sticking fingers under the edges of rocks in an attempt to move the rock.

An employee at Phantom, Jeanie from Massachusetts, received a visit from her brother. Unbeknownst to Jeanie, her brother caught a scorpion and took it out of the canyon in a sealed paper cup. Back in his room in Massachusetts, he kept the poor scorpion caged, feeding it insects.

Jeanie returned to Massachusetts to visit during Christmas. Much to her horror, she discovered the caged scorpion her brother had kidnapped from the Grand Canyon. An avid believer in leaving the environment unchanged by humans, Jeanie retrieved the scorpion from her protesting brother, put it in a cup, and carried it on her lap from Massachusetts to Arizona on the airplane. Upon her return to Phantom Ranch, she took it out the back door of the bunkhouse, knelt down and removed the lid of the cup. The well-traveled scorpion ran to a spot a few feet from that awful cup. It was on its Grand Canyon home soil at last.

Just then, a lizard ran down a tree trunk, gobbled up that scorpion, and disappeared into the fallen leaves in an environment unchanged by humans.

People fear being stung by scorpions, but I lived at Phantom Ranch for more than ten years, and only got stung twice. I am legally blind. If something appears strange to me, I automatically reach out and touch it to feel what it is.

A scorpion wouldn't like that. I was even the maintenance person one year which meant sticking my hands in all sorts of unsavory places. And yet, I never got stung on the job.

Both times I did get stung were while I slept. I was sleeping alone in my waterbed in the employee dorm. The bed was in a frame box on a pedestal. Somehow a scorpion got in bed with me, perhaps falling from the ceiling. As it was crawling down the inside of my arm, I bent my arm in my sleep. The frightened scorpion stung me on the inside of my elbow. Eventually awakened by the spreading pain and numbness, I realized that after all those years, I finally had been stung by a scorpion. I lay there for awhile wondering what I should do. Was the scorpion still in bed with me, or was it on the floor somewhere between me and my slippers? Obviously I should get out of bed with the scorpion, but my slippers were a few steps away. In my sleepy state, I was quite flummoxed. I finally got up the nerve to walk across the floor barefoot in the dark to get my slippers. I turned on the light and shook out my sheets and blankets right down to the plastic waterbed. No scorpion. I remade the bed, took a trip to the bathroom, and came back to bed. I awakened occasionally to take notice of how much the throbbing pain and numbness had spread up and down my arm. By mid-morning, the effects of the sting had spread along my whole right arm, but by that evening all of the pain and numbness had gone.

Of course, I told the other employees that there was a renegade scorpion loose in the dorm. It was found smashed right outside my door. Apparently it was trying to make a getaway when I came out my door going to the bathroom and I unknowingly stepped on

it. Fortunately I always wore something on my feet even on the way to the bathroom. That scorpion was mostly clear, an inch long, a *Centruroides sculpturatus*, or Arizona bark scorpion, supposedly the most painful of all scorpions at Grand Canyon.

Different people have different levels of tolerance to scorpion stings. One woman got stung, then ran half a mile to the ranger station. She was so distraught about being stung by a scorpion that her fast-beating heart spread the venom all through her body. She had such severe reactions that she had to be flown out of the canyon in a helicopter. She probably would have been all right if she had remained calm.

The other time I was stung was when a number of us Phantom employees camped at "The Diving Pool," about six miles up Phantom Creek. Camping there was illegal without a permit, but it was so remote that we thought there was no chance we would be caught by a Park Service ranger. I found a nice flat spot to throw down my sleeping bag and pad, right next to one of those prickly pear cactus that stands upright and tends to be a favorite lair for scorpions. In the middle of the night, a scorpion climbed up on my arm. Since my head was resting there, it stung me on my cheek. I was worried because I was in such a remote place, and the sting was pretty close to my brain. Fortunately I remained calm and the sting only caused some discomfort and swelling, neither of which prevented my return to the Ranch the next day.

I don't know anything about that scorpion but I think I saw a little Park Service arrowhead insignia on its shoulder as it stung me. Could the National Park Service have a contract with scorpions to patrol remote parts of the canyon where park rangers rarely go? Instead of a ticket, they issue pain, numbness, and swelling.

There are over 2,000 scorpion species world-wide, but only a few dozen are considered deadly. Right here in Arizona there are over 54 different species. I'm fortunate to know a world-renowned scorpion expert who allowed me to interview him.

Rich Ayrey is a Flagstaff resident who has written many scientific papers on scorpions. He has discovered and identified ten species. As a dubious high honor, he even named one after his wife. He has been studying scorpions since 1972 and has never been stung, even when collecting specimens. He said the secret is that scorpions can only sting forward. So, when he puts a container in front of the scorpion, the wary arachnid is eyeing the container while Rich gives it a poke in the rear. Voila, a captive. As I started in with my list of questions, Rich jumped up and ran to another room, returning with a variety of containers, all chock full of squirming scorpions. During his informal presentation, he would brandish one, enthusiastically explaining all about it, giving it a fond glance, and ending each presentation with, "Isn't this one cute?" I, on the other hand, have spent the better part of my life trying to avoid scorpions. By the end of the afternoon, I had a grudging respect for scorpions as master adaptors to their harsh environment and major eaters of insects. But I still plan to try to avoid them. Rich's parting comment was, "Don't be afraid of scorpions!" I still shook out my scarf as I left, just in case. Thanks to Rich for his enlightening talk.

Ancient water-dwelling scorpions found in the fossil record were over three feet long. They were probably one of the first creatures to crawl out of the water and live on dry land, surviving through and past the age of dinosaurs.

As long as 3,000 years ago, scorpions were in human cultural mythology. Persians saw them as evil spirits, Greeks saw them as a symbol of evil and death and named a constellation Scorpio. Mayans called that same constellation "Sign of the Death God." Ancient Egyptians believed in a Scorpion Goddess named Serket who had power over poisonous creatures.

The color variations, even among the same species, are quite radically different, ranging from pale yellow, almost translucent, through orange, brown, and all the way to black. Coloration depends on their habitat.

Scorpions have two main eyes on the top of their head, but also clusters of eyes on the corners of their carapace, or outer shell. Vision is not their strong sense because they are highly sensitive to light. Moonlight is just as bright to scorpions as sunlight is to humans. A more important sense comes from cells on their leg tips and hairs which helps them to feel vibrations as close as three feet. Also, pectines are organs on the underside of their abdomens which help them detect odors.

Centruroides sculpturatus, or the Arizona bark scorpion, is the only one that can be deadly in our state. Their neurotoxins cause people to have respiratory or cardiac reactions, with small children being the most vulnerable.

Scorpions are predators. They eat insects, lizards, geckos and also other scorpions. They prefer ambush predation, waiting for dinner to saunter by, grabbing small prey and eating them alive. Larger prey is subdued by the venom-filled stinger.

Ranging in size from a table knife to a thumbnail, scorpions are found from the Himalayas to the Andes, in tropical rainforests, grasslands, seashores, deserts, and caves on six continents at elevations up to 16,000 feet. Scorpion habitat is limited only by climate as the scorpion's body temperature must warm up before it can become active.

Scorpions belong to the family of arachnids, right along with spiders, ticks, and mites, because they all have eight legs, but no skeleton. An exoskeleton made of flexible, stretchy cuticle forms a waterproof carapace as a protective barrier.

The two major parts of the scorpion body are the abdomen, and the head/body part called the cephalothorax. The abdomen concludes with the tail. In front of the stinging tail is a bulbous segment called the telson, which has the glands containing the poison. Ducts carry the venom to the stinger's tip. Scorpions sting only to subdue prey or protect themselves.

The claw-like pincers in front of the head, called pedipalps, are good for burrowing and also grabbing prey. There are teeth on the outer edges. If the claws are small and weak, the venom is powerfully poisonous. Conversely, if the pincers look large and lobster-esque, the venom is weak, since the pincers can do the work alone. The mouth also contains pincers, called chelicerae, for tearing up food. Digestive fluids flow out of the mouth when food is being shredded. Meal time is a long process, and the scorpion doesn't need to eat again for several weeks. They don't travel far, so they don't need much energy. They also don't need water, because they use their prey's fluids.

Scorpion mating dance—smaller boy meets larger girl, grabs both hands (pincers) in his, and proceeds in a kind of box step dance. Touching mouth parts in a kissing motion, they might sting each other but cause no harm. The male releases a sticky spermatophore onto a flat surface, and guides his partner directly over the pile so she can readily take those male sex cells into her body. The date is over. The male skedaddles. Being the smaller of the two, he doesn't want to wait around to see if his date is hungry.

Scorpion eggs develop inside the mother's body, feeding on the yolk. Gestation ranges from two months to two years. Born alive, each baby immediately scrambles up a leg onto mama's back to join other siblings, having somewhere between 25-100 brothers and sisters. The babies are called scorplings, perhaps in an attempt to make them sound cute. If a scorpling falls off, mama stops to pick it up, recognizing her brood by scent. Born white, defenseless, with no venom or tail, they molt after a couple of weeks. Then they are equipped and ready to be on their own. They molt between five to eight more times as they grow, taking six months up to several years before they become adults.

Scientists have found scorpion venom to be helpful for some stroke victims and also for the detection of cancer cells. Scorpions are an intricate part of the food web in their habitat, helpful because they eat so many insects.

While grateful for their contributions, I still plan to shake out my shoes anytime I'm camping in the canyon.

XVIII
Water

The rocks start baking early at Phantom Ranch as soon as the sun crests the canyon wall. First, the sun blasts the cliffs on the west side of Bright Angel Creek. As the sun's position shifts higher, it aims its rays to the eastern slope. Trapped in that August oven, Keith and I needed to swim.

We left the Ranch behind, hiking north to the confluence of Bright Angel Creek and Phantom Creek. Bright Angel is deep and swiftly moving and Phantom is a quiet trickle. As we hiked in Phantom Creek, the clear, warm water came just to the top of the ratty, old pair of tennis shoes I was wearing, left at the Ranch by an unknown hiker.

We splashed our way through the creek, enjoying the small ripples, the lush vegetation along the sides, tall grasses and bright green, shady cottonwood trees overhanging the creek. Leaving behind this comforting shade, we entered an area of huge boulders and narrow cliff faces rising sharply vertical. No rock climbing here! The boulder jumble created delightful pools, three to four feet in depth, into which we gratefully flung ourselves, luxuriating in the water's embrace. Still feeling the morning heat, we were grateful when the sun disappeared behind a series of cooling grey clouds.

We lounged decadently in the pools until our fingers turned pruney, finally hoisting ourselves out to dry off and munch our lunch. After sharing a peach, we decided it would be prudent to head back, given that it was, after all, monsoon season.

From our narrow perspective of sheer cliffs on either side of us, we had no idea what was transpiring on the North Rim. There, at nine thousand feet at the apex of the Kaibab Plateau angry, black clouds coalesced. The thunderheads unleashed a monstrous deluge that crashed violently through sun-baked arroyos, dictated by gravity and squeezed by narrow cliffs. Phantom Canyon offered an outlet for this fury.

Downstream Keith and I slowly picked our way back through the gentle creek, Keith joking that footholds seemed scarce in the smooth, towering cliffs. From where we were, a quarter-mile of creek was easy to see behind us before it curved away into the canyon's depths.

At the same instant I saw it, Keith heard it.

"FLOOD – RUN!" he screamed.

With his long legs and lanky frame Keith managed to shimmy up on a ledge—probably the only one for miles. Stunned by the sight, I experienced an incredible lesson in the power of water. With no opportunity to escape, I was picked up and tossed into the red, debris-filled four foot wall of water. It caught me at chest level and carried me along like I was a twig.

I was filled with images of an unassembled puzzle:

*Amazement that this violent intruder had rolled right on top of the gentle three inch deep Phantom Creek

*What will happen to Keith

*My own terror of being dragged down to the creek bottom, my left leg impaled, then popping me up to the surface, a bobbing cork amid the crashing boulders, branches and roiling water

*I could die

Keith appeared in my field of vision, yelling and trying to pick his way along the edge toward me without falling in. I yelled back and managed to octopus myself around a boulder miraculously still anchored to the bank. Stationary momentarily, Keith found me – and with great effort – was able to extract me from the raging torrent.

We collapsed, exhausted, on the tiny spit of sand between the current and the sheer cliff—only to leap up quickly as red ants scurried over us. They, too, had been displaced by the flash flood and were looking for safety. We watched, still panting, as motorcycle-sized boulders tumbled in the current. Shaky, but OK, except for cuts and bruises, we waited with the ants for the flood to subside.

Several hours later, still marooned on our tiny spit of sand, we cautiously measured the height of the creek. It was knee level on me. No more big rocks rolled through. We began our slow return, amazed at how everything had changed—rocks displaced here, logs jammed there, vegetation stripped bare away from what used to be the creek's bank, now a ravaged edge of crumbling dirt.

Arriving back at the Ranch in the dark, we were met by worried Ranchers who had seen the Bright Angel Creek turn an ugly color, choked with debris.

Years later, during the Northern Arizona Writing Project, Ranger Jacob led us on the Dynamic Earth hike. He asked us to close our eyes to experience the most powerful force on Earth, then playfully squirted each of us with a gentle mist of water.

But, I know what that force can REALLY do. This is one force that you DON'T want to be with you. It's a reminder that we are all at the mercy of a powerful, indifferent natural world.

PART II

XIX
Antarctica

We journeyed to Antarctica, the navel of Mother Earth. Raw, stark. Jutting black monuments of rock push out of the snow, forming jagged mountain ridges without a shred of vegetation. Glaciers shove between two sheer cliffs and appear at the shoreline as a towering wall of ice. Time, water, wind, precipitation, and extreme temperatures have been at work on this land for eons. Yet it looks newly scrubbed, fresh—unsullied by humans. Snowflakes here can be the size of CDs. Sea ice, held fast to the land, doubles the size of the continent every winter, exceeding more than twice the size of the United States. Enormous tabular icebergs shear off in the spring, eventually grounding in a cove or melting out at sea. While the Arctic is ocean surrounded by land, Antarctica is a huge land mass surrounded by ocean. It's almost as if there were a depression at the North Pole causing a bulge at the South Pole.

Eyes stay riveted to the magnificent scenery, that raw beauty of nature. A Lindblad Cove glacier sheared off as we watched, causing a tremendous splash, and sent our huge cruise ship bobbing. The women standing behind me spontaneously burst into the National Geographic theme song, which had been running through my head all day.

We disembarked for a walk on the fast ice, struck silent by the majesty of the 360° view of mountains, rocks, ice, glaciers, and blue skies. Clouds hovered around jagged peaks as if someone had tossed a fluffy, white scarf. There were seals, skuas, giant petrels, and of course, the on-going antics of the penguins, all just several yards away.

We kayaked in aptly-named Paradise Bay. The fastest hour and a half of the trip was spent idyllically paddling around in our circular world of mountains and icebergs. Spring ice is unstable and constantly changing, so we witnessed icebergs turning over. Booming avalanches roared, sent up clouds of snow and scoured new paths downslope. Walls of ice broke from the landmass and crashed into the sea. Huge icebergs created hanging icicles that dripped on the mirror-like water, creating a sound like a gurgling creek.

All was blissfully serene until we were attacked by a rogue band of Vikings. Fortunately it turned out to be the bar staff from the ship in Viking horn hats and bearing grog.

The light is breathtaking. Sunrise was around 2:27 a.m., sunset 11:12 p.m. In-between, the sky became a peachy orange-pink, dramatic against all the icy whiteness and black mountain peaks, throwing the soft light on tabular icebergs as we passed by.

After we crossed back over the treacherous Drake Passage, Cape Horn appeared, that southernmost hunk of rock marking the end, or depending upon your point of view, the beginning of South America. Graveyard to countless ships, the huge rock face juts upwards to the steely grey skies. Low clouds scudded across the land, with one lone snowcapped peak of the Andes spot-lit by a sunbeam far in the distance.

PENGUINS: ANTARCTICA'S LITTLE PEOPLE

A penguin is on the trail from his rookery of exposed rock and dirt to the ocean. A human inadvertently stands on the penguin highway. The penguin, flippers thrust behind for balance while walking, stops abruptly, flummoxed by this human obstruction. (Not the sharpest tack in the box of birds.) Penguins have the right of way, so the human moves, and the penguin resumes his waddling gait to the sea.

They often trip, sprawling beak-first into the snow, then lie there for a moment, as if embarrassed and hoping no other penguins noticed. Becoming upright again requires much wriggling and flipper flapping, followed by much waddling and tobogganing, or scooting around on their bellies.

One time, some of the ship's staff went out to test the ice for stability, leaving orange traffic cones where it was safe to walk. A gaggle of penguins waddled over, surrounded the cones and conversed amongst themselves as to the origins and possible IQ of this new addition to their landscape. What kind of penguins were those orange cones, anyway?

It was spring nesting time under grey skies, and the greatest gift possible from the male to the female is a rock to help build up the nest. One male, obviously an overachiever, wrestled over an enormous rock. His mate raised her eyebrow, wondering where to put such a behemoth. Other males brought their mates more sensible-sized rocks, much cooed over and pushed carefully into just the right spot. One male brought a small snowball, which was scoffed at and rejected.

Penguins swim toward the shore and jump out of the water in one swift motion. Amazingly, they usually arrive upright or else scoot around on their bellies with flippers and clawed feet providing locomotion. Although they don't fly, they have evolved to "fly through the water." They swim with their flippers, not their feet, just above the water line using a technique called porpoising—swimming rapidly just below the surface, then propelling upwards in a low arc for a quick breath.

There really are only two kinds of penguins—the white ones coming toward you, and the black ones going away from you, a contrast present in all penguin species. All that is needed to complete the tuxedo ensemble would be a snazzy bowtie and cummerbund. We actually saw four kinds – the gentoo, the Adelie, the chinstrap and the emperor. Although amazing that any of these species can survive here, the brushtails, including the gentoo, Adelie and chinstrap, spend winters in the 28° seawater and on ice floes, coming to land only in the spring and summer for breeding and raising their young. The regals – four foot tall, 90-pound emperors have the true Antarctic existence, raising their young on the continent in midwinter at 70° below. The males stand stoically with the egg on their feet, brood pouch keeping it warm, for two months in the dead of winter while their ladies are out feeding at sea. The males huddle together in the howling 100-mph Antarctic winds. Grey fluffy chicks are born right as the moms return to take over. The relieved and emaciated males head out to sea to eat, but soon return to help with the feedings, trudging back and forth to the sea. Chicks can eat up to two pounds of regurgitated fish and squid in one feeding. Finally the chick is able to feed on its own during the height of the summer bounty.

Penguins are barometers of climate change. As Antarctica is one of the first places to experience changing conditions, it's important to notice what is going on in the penguin colonies. The increasing length of the summers combined with rising temperatures have affected the normal migration of gentoos, causing them to head farther south than ever before observed. Emperors have been noted farther north than before. And the chinstraps have burgeoned in numbers due to the increase in open water where their natural habitat has less sea ice now.

LEOPARD SEALS AREN'T YOUR AVERAGE SEAL.

These aren't the cute kind of seal that looks like it should be bouncing a ball on its nose. It's a top predator, known to attack Zodiacs, (a rubber raft) kayaks and people, sometimes leaping out of the water and into a boat. Imagine suddenly having an extra passenger with gnashing teeth who is eleven feet long and weighs 1,300 pounds. Leopard seals, so called because of the black spots on the chin and belly, haul out to rest on ice floes, but otherwise stay in the frigid water, prowling. Its primitive-looking huge head with a large hump atop a skinny neck doesn't seem to match its long, slender body. But that huge reptilian head helps it to swallow its favorite meal whole—penguins. They also eat krill, fish, squid, and other seals.

Unlike most seal species which congregate gregariously, the leopard seal is solitary. Mothers give birth to a single five foot long pup out on the ice floes. Leopard seals range widely, migrating to the southern most parts of South America, Africa, Australia, and New Zealand. Their locomotion on land resembles a caterpillar, only much faster.

Think of the vastness of the great Southern Ocean, swirling clockwise around the continent of Antarctica, sloshing into the Pacific and Atlantic oceans, thus affecting us all. Antarctica should be what we look for first on a map or globe, our global center, the navel. What happens in Antarctica affects the rest of the world, and what happens

124

in the rest of the world affects Antarctica. Antarctica proves that we are all one. If we were to lose the Antarctic Ice Cap, sea levels would rise worldwide up to 330 feet. Just look at the coastlines of all the other continents to see what that would mean. We would be wise to care for this vast, magnificent wilderness, this last unspoiled place, as if our very lives depend upon it. Because, really—they do.

XX
Australia

The plane circled over the sprawling lights of Los Angeles before heading out to sea. Then there was only the occasional pinprick of light below, indicating the presence of a huge cargo freighter chugging across the Pacific. Fifteen hours later, we saw lights again; this time the lights of Sydney, Australia. We had a new respect for the enormity of our planet. Before landing, we watched the most magnificent sunrise, a brilliant orange right over the water. As it rose up and away from the horizon, the color became green—light lime green. Truly an amazing color to welcome us to this hemisphere.

We headed up into the Blue Mountains outside of Sydney on a sparkling summer's day, but unfortunately there were tremendous bush fires caused by hooligans and further fueled by hat-snatching winds. The vegetation is incredible, with tree ferns dating back to the Jurassic. It's the eucalyptus, or gum trees that burn so violently, because of the natural volatile oils in the leaves.

So, it was onto Tasmania. Although it was still summer, we were much farther south. "We get all our weather systems straight from Antarctica!" said Crocodile Dundee. Actually, his name was Mike, but he had the hat, the coat, the looks, and the accent. The weather changed to cool and rainy. These little storms came out of nowhere, deposited drenching rains, followed by sun, and then more rain. Our lodge was on the edge of Cradle Lake at the base of Cradle Mountain, the snow line a mere one hundred feet above our heads. Even with the mist and drizzle, it was mighty spectacular. The mountain peaks rose in great fins, showing the scraping and gouging of glaciers all the way down to the lake. The snowcapped peaks wavered in and out of the shifty, gauzy rainclouds. Two big waterfall systems tumbled down from the heights above, rivers wending their way through a dense and mossy forest, water the color of coffee from all the tannins in the grasses.

The most delightful surprise right out our back porch were small wallabies. The local name for them is Tasmanian "pademelons." They hopped about, totally unconcerned with us gawking Yanks. They were beyond cute when they stood up on their back legs and fiddled in their pouch, looking for all the world like the absent-minded professor searching for glasses or a pocket watch. Sometimes a pademelon would shoot up its head if we made a noise, survey us, and bound off. All marsupials in the kangaroo family can be tending three babies at once: a joey in the pouch, one old enough to be out of the pouch, and one in utero. Mamas also produce fat-rich milk for the out-of-the-pouch joey, and simultaneously carbohydrate rich milk for the one still in the pouch. The late sunsets at around 9 p.m. made for long, wonderful hours of wildlife viewing.

On a night spotlighting tour we saw nocturnal wombats. They were quite a surprise, so big, between 40 and 70 pounds and 48 inches long. Fossil records show that originally there were hippo-sized wombats. They look bear-ish, like koalas, with the same white-tipped ears. Unlike true bears, they are herbivores, not omnivores. They dine on grass, roots, and fungi. Wombats have round, close-to-the-ground bodies, with powerful legs for digging their 100-foot burrows complete with antechambers. A backwards facing pouch prevents a pocket full of dirt and a sputtering baby.

More aggressive are the brush-tailed possums. One actually charged Keith as we headed back to our cabin after dinner. These are not to be confused with New World opossums. These cat-sized creatures only weigh eleven pounds, but when threatened, they rear up to their full 23 inches and screech. They have a raccoon-like waddle, with a prehensile tail that sticks out, rat-like, from under its other big, bushy tail. These are mostly herbivores, using their long, sharp claws to climb trees and occasionally eat young birds.

At the Melbourne airport, I wandered about holding a photo of my Australian pen pal, Jennifer. After years of corresponding, we were finally coming to Australia, so could she possibly meet us for dinner? She briskly wrote back that, No, she would meet us at the airport and take us home with her. So I laughed when I noticed a woman walking toward me also holding a photograph. First, she informed us that we were off to the golf course. My husband and I glanced nervously at each other, anxious not to cause a faux pas and get off on the wrong foot with these kind people. "Um," I said. "We don't play golf." "Oh, no," Jennifer responded. "We're off to see the roos! It's the best place!" And, she was right. There, looking for all the world like they should be holding a nine iron, were dozens of kangaroos, waiting for someone to yell "FORE!", congregating and hopping about on the public golf course. Some of them stood as tall as my 6' 2" husband. Talk about hazards!

Red kangaroos are the largest of the 61 species in the kangaroo/wallaby family, weighing upwards to 180 pounds. Fortunately, they are grass eaters, herding together in large groups called mobs. If threatened, they tend to bolt away in opposite directions, thus befuddling a predator. That classic kangaroo has enormous, soft feet, and huge ears. It can hop thirty feet in one bounce, cruising along at thirty mph, tail strung out behind for counterbalance. Camel-like, they can survive in all parts of Australia because they don't need much water and can eat dry, tough plants. In their grazing position, their short forelimbs are on the ground, with that muscular tail helping them balance.

In the evening we went to the dairy farm of Jennifer and her husband Horst's daughter, Janine. Janine's husband took us out spotlighting for roos after dinner. This involved us thrashing around in the back of a pickup truck holding a huge spotlight, while following the bouncing mob of kangaroos through the pastures. Included in the mob was one mama with a joey's head peeking out of her pouch. Males will box each other to compete for females. Kangaroos usually spend the afternoons dozing. Mama dumps the joey out for her nap, and the joey clamors to get back in. During the birth process, the tiny lima bean-sized infant must "swim" through the mama's fur from the birth canal to get to the pouch where the teats are.

At picnic grounds in the United States, flocks of sparrows or jays often swoop in to snatch crumbs. In Aussie parks, a much larger bird, the six-foot-tall emu comes in for leftovers. They are difficult to shoo away with just a backhand wave. One emu entered the picnic area fortunately just as we were leaving. These flightless birds can run up to thirty mph in short bursts and travel up to eight miles a day.

The emu has an unusual parenting arrangement. The female lays the eggs and then walks away, her job done. It's the males who incubate and attend the chicks.

Koalas like to hang out in eucalyptus trees, close to their larder of gum leaves. Their habitat is only a narrow band of the southern and eastern portion of the continent. It's impossible not to "ooh and ahh" while watching mama cradle her baby. A joey will stay in the pouch up to seven months, then ride on mama's back until the next joey appears. We also heard the grunt-like bellow of a mating call, and actually saw one male throw back his head as he sounded off. A distant howling brought us through the woods wondering what could possibly be making such a racket. It was a koala fight between two males.

Inactive twenty hours a day, they use their opposable thumb and three fingers with sharp claws to cling to branches of the gum trees. Since the leaves are so fibrous and difficult to digest, koalas have to eat soil or gravel like birds do to aid with digestion. Koalas are a threatened species due to destruction of their habitat and devastating bush fires. They are also hunted for their soft fur.

We saw one echidna. Echidnas are prickly footballs with short spines and a long, skinny snout. They are among the rare monotremes

©Val Jesse

130

—mammals who lay eggs. They won't run away when threatened, but rather dig with their powerful claws or roll into a tailless spiny ball. They go after ants and termites with their seven-inch tongue, pushing that long nose into a nest. After the eggs are hatched, mama nurses with milk the color of a strawberry milkshake, which oozes from pores, because they have no teats. Once the babies are too prickly for the pouch, mama unceremoniously dumps the now mature young out into the burrow.

Aboriginal occupation of Australia dates back 50,000 years. Much of their lore and knowledge was lost as tribal units were decimated after interfacing with European settlers. James Cook discovered the island continent in 1770. "If it doesn't move, chop it down" was the English motto during the colonization period, forever altering the Australian landscape. Since 1840, there has been a 66% loss of all the natural woodlands of acacia, mallee, eucalyptus, red cedar, and kauri.

Since European settlement, Australia has lost more mammal species than any other country, mostly within the first few decades of colonization. Most tragic was loss of the thylacine, commonly called the Tasmanian tiger. Grazing and farming are hard on this fragile continent with thin topsoil, which is totally unsuited to hooved placental mammals that destroy native grasses. Inappropriately imported mammals such as rabbits denuded all the grass and burrowed into the valuable, slender topsoil layer, becoming a plague on the land. Cane toads are another non-native species which have devastated native small animal populations, as they have no predators and eat anything and everything.

Rarely has such a unique, fragile landscape been so abused in relatively modern times. Fortunately, Australians and their government have taken a long hard look at their rapacious past and have begun the slow process of making amends and moving the country towards conservation and rehabilitation, while providing opportunities for the aboriginal populations. National parks and other reserves are being created and maintained.

And that's good news, mate.

XXI
Peru

A land of wild extremes: narrow coastal deserts; Andean glacial highlands; dense and steamy Amazon jungles. Peru, three times the size of California, fascinates scholars and tourists both with an enticing prehistoric and historic record. The whole country is awash with stunning archeological sites, magnificent archeoastronomy, and a long pre-Incan period. The walled Chimu city of Chan Chan is a site to rival some structures produced by the much later Incas. The relatively brief flourishing of the Inca created the most famous site of all, Machu Picchu. All this cultural richness came to a screeching halt in 1532 with the invasion, slaughter, and enslavement of millions by the Spanish conquistadors. The overlay of pagan and indigenous beliefs woven into the imposed Spanish Catholicism makes a cultural fabric as raucous as a Sunday at the Pisac Market.

The Andes Mountains are jagged, craggy, and snow-capped. They're rough, angular and sharp—as if they just jutted out of the Earth and pierced the sky. Glaciers nestle around the tallest peaks and slide into deep ravines. Clouds float, then drape around high rock monuments, dropping as a shroud, then just as quickly, rise and expose the breath-taking view again.

Within this spectacle of nature, we started our tour of culture and archaeology in this country just a few degrees off the equator. There are frequent earthquakes, causing damage to everything but the Incan stones. Wildlife was not in plentiful evidence. But there's a good animal story, nonetheless.

My husband Keith is one of those try-anything-once kind of guys. When alpaca steak appeared on the menu, of course, he had to try it. His assessment was that it was somewhat beef-like, but with a lighter taste.

The Pisac market is an experience in cultural immersion. The plaza is a garish rainbow of eye-popping color, with textiles ranging from pink, sun-scorched yellow, or sunset orange to the deepest of indigos. The Quechua women wear their bowler hats draped in scarves depicting their marital status, and wear layers of skirts and shawls amid piles of potatoes in every possible hue. We wandered, perusing the amazing displays. All around us Quechua, Spanish, English, German, and Italian voices joined the symphony of colors.

Needing a break from the press of the throng, we pulled away from the main part of the market, and walked uphill to a smaller and quieter section of stalls. A man sat before an immense loom under a shelter, working on a gorgeous tapestry filled with images of llamas and Incan gods. In my broken Spanish, I asked if we could step closer so my husband could better see his work. The man spoke some English, and invited us in. But he said "Be careful of the baby." I looked wildly around for a wrapped bundle or a baby carrier, so Keith wouldn't accidently step on an infant with his Size 13s. But instead, from around the corner of the loom came a three-week-old pure white alpaca. It bleated pathetically, and came over to rub its head against our legs and beg to be petted. Its fur was incredibly soft, and it looked right up into my face and twitched its cute little black nose and batted its fabulously long eyelashes, wriggling its way into my heart. Keith spent a long time petting the creature, and shaking his head.

"Remember that alpaca steak I tried the other night? Can't order that again," Keith said, giving the alpaca a final pat.

South American camelids were domesticated perhaps 4000 to 5000 years ago. There are still the wild versions, the vicuna and the guanaco, which take refuge in the high Andes, while the alpaca and llama are domesticated. All species are engineered to exist at high altitudes. Like camels, they are able to go long periods without water. They are grazers of grasses and plants.

Vicunas are the smallest, 39 inches at the shoulder. I was totally happy with my soft alpaca sweater I bought at the Pisac Market, until one shop owner let me feel a small swatch of vicuna fur. I gasped. It was the softest thing I have ever felt, and indeed, it turns out it is the world's finest wool. Only the Inca kings were allowed to wear it. In

Incan times, vicuna wool was harvested by hand, as well as feet, as a swift runner tackled the animal, plucked off its fleece and allowed the vicuna to go free. This ensured a steady supply of wool, as well as a vicuna able to reproduce. Today, herds are rounded up in the spring, captured, sheared, and released. Even so, vicunas can be shorn about every third year, only yielding a small amount of wool each time. They reproduce slowly, only one baby at a time, called a cria, and not necessarily every year. Illegal hunting and habitat destruction have decimated populations, but refuges are being created.

Guanacos are bigger, up to four feet tall. They are found mostly in the southern reaches of the Andes, all the way down to Tierra del Fuego. They are also considered endangered, but are not used for their wool. Their babies are called chulengos.

Llamas astonished the Spanish conquistadors for their usefulness to carry heavy loads; but also as food and fur, although their fur is very coarse. They are social creatures, herding together. There is a resident herd at Machu Picchu. One might casually peer with head and neck over the edge of a ruin, or a herd might amble by, allowing the stroking of their thick, heavy fur. A baby might suddenly realize it was the only quadruped in the area, kicking out its legs and swaying its head in a wobble with its effort to rejoin the safety of the herd.

Alpacas are about half the size of a llama, weighing in at 145 pounds, and as tall as six and a half feet at the head, three feet at the shoulder. Since they are so much smaller, alpacas are not used as beasts of burden. They have been bred for their soft woolly fur. Alpacas can be shorn every other year, and produce a greater yield, in addition to being domesticated and more numerous.

Theories abound about the genealogy of these four Andean animals. A likely scenario is alpacas derive from matings between domesticated llamas and guanacos or vicunas. Llamas may be the domesticated form of guanacos. All possible cross-breedings have been attempted, and all combinations produce fertile offspring.

Whatever their origins, I just wish I had bought more of those gorgeous alpaca textiles at the Pisac Market.

XXII
Whale

On a cruise of the Inside Passage in Alaska, we traveled with Lindblad, highly valued for its small ships and equally small passenger complement. Because there were only sixty of us, the ship often pulled over to off-the-beaten-track islands, untrodden by humans, where we would hike. That's a tough thing to do in Alaska, because of the boggy muskeg and horrific devil's claw.

But my absolute favorite experience was pulling into shore by Zodiac, (a rubber raft) unloading the kayaks, then exploring the shorelines with ease, watching the dense vegetation of pine trees and shrubby, prickly undergrowth from water level. Several of the ship's staff watched over us from their Zodiacs, because grizzly bears were in the area.

When I get into a kayak, my French-Canadien roots take over, and I become a Voyageur, exploring North America for the first time by canoe. I found my rhythm, dipping the paddle from side to side, doing that small twist at the waist on the follow-through. I became one with my oar, the boat, and the water, falling into a meditative trance. So I was startled out of my reverie when a Zodiac zoomed straight towards us, the driver gesticulating wildly. When she was close enough, she cut the motor.

"Didn't you see that?" she yelled in alarm.

"See what?" Keith and I responded in unison. Keith is blind, so it made sense to put him in the front so I could steer from the back. The only problem with that arrangement is that I am 5'1" and Keith is 6'2". So, while I could see everything on either side, all I could see in front of me was his lifejacket.

"You were paddling right into the gaping maw of a humpback whale!"

Our reality shifted. Along the left side of our tiny craft only twenty feet away, a huge undulation broke the surface. The grey back of a whale rose, then sank. It glided by us slowly, all sixty feet of it, raising its head for a blow, waiting politely with the exhale until it had already passed us. We watched it with silent and humbled awe.

In the Alaskan summer evening, there's still plenty of light at 10:30. We were out on the deck admiring the shifting hues of orange in the clouds when there was a commotion off the port bow. We rushed forward to see a large battalion of humpback whales milling about, taking shallow dives, spouting, then going down until the massive tail was all that was left above the water. With a curl and a flip, that, too, disappeared. Then the slow rise of the back showed off that small fin. The pectoral flippers rose up, playfully slapping the water. Then, an abrupt change. They tightened their group, bouncing at the surface with their huge heads pointed at the sky. "They're going to bubble feed!" one of our guides shouted, as he ran to drop an underwater microphone. The whales disappeared, but we could hear their soundings through the hydrophone. Forming a "bubble net,"

they spiraled upwards, trapping a large group of fish inside a screen of bubbles, and driving them upwards. There came a huge moan, and the entire group of whales rose as one, mouths agape, devouring the flailing fish. The captain cut the motor, threw out the anchor, and we watched this incredible cooperative group feeding for over an hour. Finally, even the Alaskan summer sun was setting with a pinkish glow and we could see the whales no more. But we could hear the mighty whoosh of their spray as we pulled away.

In Antarctica we also witnessed humpbacks, crossing paths with a mama and her baby, seeing and hearing their breathy blow, watching their rising backs, slapping pectoral fins and graceful tail flukes.

Humpbacks have accordion-like grooved pleats in their necks for swallowing massive amounts of water during lunge-feeding, then pushing out the water like a sieve through their baleen plates with their huge tongue, trapping fish, krill, and other microorganisms for a trip down to the stomach. Instead of teeth, these whales have baleen plates hanging from their upper 13-foot-wide jaw, made out of the same material as human fingernails and hair. Their 350 baleen plates can each be up to 31 inches long. Ironically, these enormous creatures survive on the tiniest of organisms—just lots of them. Since their food source lives within 100 feet or so from the surface, that's where these filter feeders tend to stay. They dive from four to forty minutes, tail disappearing dramatically, then return with a mighty blow. Weighing in at over forty tons, the acrobatic humpbacks are a marvel to watch. They love to breach, flinging their 62 foot long bodies completely out of the ocean and returning to the water with a thunderous splash. When whales exchange air, they empty 90% of their lungs compared with only 15% for the average human. Humpback exhale is called "a blow." When the classic "thar she blows" occurs, it is over nine feet in height, showing across the water as a wide and bushy fountain. They have the longest pectoral fins that are almost one third their body length. They laze about on the surface, slapping those long, scalloped edges like wings. Each whale can be uniquely identified by coloration and markings on the underside of the tail.

Humpback males are famous for their songs, audible for hundreds of miles, since sound travels five times faster in water than air. Hanging upside down while singing, snout pointed to the ocean floor, the male produces low frequency moans, bellows, grunts, chirps and squeals. Each song has two to nine main stanzas, and are sung in the same order, but with constant improvisation. Since these songs are performed at the breeding grounds, perhaps there is a link to their four-footed ancestors like the elk, who make a dolphin-like bugling sound to attract their mates.

Humpbacks are in the rorqual class of whales. Rorquals cover a lot of planetary distance with migrations from both polar regions where they feed, to the warmer equatorial waters where they breed and raise their young.

Their blubber layer helps to keep them warm in the 29° polar waters. Humpbacks follow a predictable migration journey with seasonal timing. The streamlined whales move with little resistance, racking up 12,500 miles of migration from Antarctica to the Arctic using both Pacific and Atlantic routes. Some of these large baleen whales can live up to 100 years.

Besides humpbacks, orcas also swam alongside the ships in both our Alaska and Antarctica voyages, mostly just mamas and babies. Traveling in pods, occasionally a 30-foot-long male surfaced, startling us with his 6-foot dorsal fin slicing the surface majestically, then breaching, showing off those half-moon white spots by the dorsal fin and eyes. There is also a grey saddle marking on their behinds. These close-knit pods of up to four generations hug the coastal waters where they feed on schooling fish.

The orcas and also dolphins are toothed whales, because they are hunters. They use echolocation as a means of navigation, communicating with whistles, clicks and calls, each pod with a distinctive dialect of sounds. They specialize in "spyhopping," rising up so that head and pectoral fins are thrust through the surface, scoping out the above-water area. Some orca pods stay as residents in a particular area, while others live a transient existence. They are the fastest marine mammal swimmers at 34 mph. They are completely

"Whales at Play"

supported by the water which makes them weightless, so strandings on shore are dangerous. Orcas have been observed lunging onto shore in pursuit of sea lion pups off the coast of South America, then wriggling back into the water—a hazardous move. Pods have even been seen attacking blue whales, the largest animal ever to have lived on our planet. Orcas work cooperatively, with one throwing itself over the blue's blowhole while the others attack, earning them the nickname, "killer whale." In Antarctica they work cooperatively to tip over ice floes where seals have hauled themselves out.

On a Zodiac cruise in Antarctica, we caught a fleeting glimpse of three minke whales. We gave a merry parallel chase, but stayed a respectful distance away, and still we were able to spot them several times.

Minke whales have a distinctive white stripe on their flippers. Minkes are diminutive compared to their fellow rorquals, the humpbacks. Minkes are only 31 feet long. They tend to stay in a specified area and adapt to the available food source, and tend to be loners.

Fifty million years ago, cetaceans began the pull away from their hoofed mammal relatives, probably starting out as fish eaters in rivers and shallow lagoons, later making an amphibious transition. Today's sheep and cattle are the closest relatives to dolphins and whales. Ancient marine areas have shifted as the continents drifted, exposing whale fossils in such diverse places as India, Pakistan, and Antarctica.

Lore and awe of whales harkens back to biblical times with the story of Jonah. Prehistoric coastal inhabitants must have rejoiced in the occasional carcass that washed ashore, and found a use for every scrap of the whale from flukes to skull. Whale bones became rafters, and Vikings were known for making chairs from whale vertebrae.

Sparing the reader the details, the modern whaling industry, with its heyday in the 1800s, was and still is brutal. Products from the slaughtered whales went from the absurdities of ladies' corsets, umbrella ribs and fishing rods, to the more practical use of whale oil for lamps and candles before electricity. The slaughter reduced global populations to levels from which some species never recovered. Humpback populations estimated at 250,000 prior to massive whaling are now closer to 18,000.

Thanks to world-wide efforts of the International Whaling Commission, (IWC) only three countries continue commercial whaling: Norway, Iceland, and Japan. Japan claims to be whaling for "scientific" purposes, but observations by Greenpeace indicate otherwise. 51 previous whaling countries now honor the cessation on whaling. Antarctica has been declared a Southern Ocean Whale Sanctuary by the IWC, a claim Japan blatantly ignores. Japan currently targets minke whales.

Bequia, a small island in the Caribbean, is allowed two humpbacks per year for their native fishery. Indigenous populations with historic links to whaling continue to take whales, but at a decided disadvantage for the whales. By using modern weaponry such as harpoons loaded with bombs, motorized boats and airplanes instead of a single hunter in a kayak with a harpoon, whale populations are still struggling. Additionally, incidental by-catch by commercial fishing gillnets and driftnets take a tremendous toll, particularly on dolphins.

Today's biggest threat to whales is pollution. Plastics, oil, chemicals, and sewage are awash, forming oceanic dead zones. Pollution from industry and agriculture accumulates in the blood stream of these top-of-the-food-chain eaters. When food is scarce the body metabolizes fat all at once and the toxic overload can kill. Noise pollution from ships, military boats, oil and gas drilling, and sonar wreak havoc on the tiny crystals in the whale's brain that are a part of their navigation system and function as internal compasses. This can cause whales to end up stranding far off course.

Captive cetaceans, particularly in for-profit marine parks are currently surrounded by a swirl of controversy. Fortunately, some parks are ending their captive breeding programs for orcas. With whale watching expeditions and wonderful ways of using technology to observe them in their own environment, is it really necessary to take these magnificent creatures from the wild and confine them in miserable enclosures?

Establishing marine protected areas as critical habitat sanctuaries for feeding and calving is necessary for whale survival. Let's return to the mindset of First Nation peoples who watch these fellow intelligent mammals with respect and awe. Whales are the Earth's truly global citizens, and need the depth and breadth of the ocean to be free from human interference. With 70% of the Earth's surface covered with ocean, surely there is room for us all.

XXIII
Sea Turtle

I received the call over spring break. I'm sure my mother planned it that way, waiting until we were all the way to Hawaii, too far away to rush back to her bedside. Then she let her life quietly slip away, ridding herself of that horrible kidney cancer.

I was an only child with a military father gone much of the time, and my mother was the person I was closest to on this earth. She just couldn't be gone, but the last time I saw her, I knew it would be the last time. The silence was so loud without her.

I staggered out into the Hawaiian sunshine, beside myself with grief. The sound of crashing waves and roaring surf engulfed me. The soothing rhythm coaxed me to stop at a rock to sit on the edge of the cliff and just stare into the green water flecked with foam. Wait – something was moving in the water. A sea turtle, with a back as large as a human torso, came up for air, nibbling on something, perhaps a piece of algae. It just bobbed there elegantly, allowing the waves to chart its course, not fighting the current, just going with the flow, gently making corrections, its fore flippers forming a figure eight as it glided majestically. From my perspective it seemed to fly through the water as I watched from my perch above. And watch, I did. The turtle guided me through my grief with its sapience and grace, how it trusted in its watery universe, no fighting, just small movements, feeling the rhythm of life, coming up for air, resting, eating and basking in the sun. It was exactly what I needed to understand—that life can go on, it's OK to be alone in the world, and all important opportunities will present themselves eventually. Go with the flow, Nancy.

Green turtles are the lawnmowers of ocean citizens, cropping seagrasses to aid in that ecosystem's health by stimulating new growth and nutrition for the sea creatures of that habitat. They are the "bison" of the underwater grasslands, with a jaw that has a serrated edge for easy grass trimming. They are the largest of the hard-shelled sea turtles, up to 650 pounds and 47 inches long. The scutes, or scales, which cover the shell and skin, are smooth and streamlined for effortless movement in water. They are gorgeous "gardeners" of the sea.

On the Caribbean island of Bequia, we visited a sea turtle sanctuary for hawksbills. Their narrow bill, shaped in a perpetual grimace, gives this sea turtle its name. An old man now, the proprietor told his story as a hunter of sea turtles, formerly proud of the thousands he killed. Hawksbills are not edible due to their toxic diet, since they consume only sponges, which are basically sea glass. This hunter killed these turtles for the famous "tortoiseshell" ornaments. The scutes of the hawksbill are overlapping and easy to tear apart and make into eyeglasses or combs or jewelry. Over time, our host said, it got harder and harder to find these turtles. Finally, visiting scientists informed the island's residents that these turtles would probably go extinct very soon because of overhunting. So now, in a race against time to save the species, he vowed to do everything he could to insure hawksbills were protected. He spoke through tears in his eyes for his part in their slaughter and undoing. The sanctuary provided breeding areas, safe places for the females to lay eggs, protected areas for the eggs to naturally incubate in the sand, and seawater tanks for different ages of hatchlings and young turtles to mature before being released. I approached one of the tanks with platter-sized turtles swimming from one end to the other. As one came by, I couldn't resist, I reached out to stroke the shell. The turtle stopped, turned and glared at me, as if to say – "How dare you? Haven't you humans done enough damage?" After a lingering and thoroughly accusatory stare, it resumed its stately course around the tank. Thoroughly chastised, I kowtowed and respected its existence and right to be here.

Hawksbills weigh in at around 190 pounds and are about 40 inches long. Their gorgeous coloration of cream, chocolate, yellow, amber and brown in fan-shaped patterns over their carapace was their downfall, making them attractive for trinket-making. Their bill is perfectly shaped for plucking sponges from coral reefs. They are crucial to the reef habitat, because they keep the sponges in check. Sponges and coral are in constant competition for space, with the former dominating. But when hawksbill populations are in balance, they chomp their way through the overabundant sponges, which allows coral reefs to flourish. And world-wide, coral reefs are endangered by a variety of pollutants and they need hawksbills to help maintain that ecosystem.

Visiting Mazatlan, Mexico, we witnessed where the government operates an excellent turtle recovery program for olive ridleys. When a nesting female comes ashore to scrape a pit in the sand to dig her nest, she lays up to 100 leathery eggs the size of ping pong balls. Without looking back after covering them, she returns to the sea. It's a good thing she doesn't look back, because what she would see is Mexican scientists digging up the eggs and carting them off for protection, recreating the nest in safety until two to three months later when the hatchlings emerge. Because female sea turtles return by instinct to the very beach where they hatched as babies, these tiny new turtles are brought back to the exact location. Except now, they need help from us tourists. We each were handed a wriggly little black turtle, a two-inch baby olive ridley. A line in the sand, literally, directed us where NOT to step. And in small groups, we each brought our baby ridley forward so it could begin its life in the sea. Only one in 1,000 turtle eggs live to adulthood. They have to get to the ocean without first being consumed by a predator while still an egg on the beach. Getting into the water is a challenge in itself.

We watched the hatchlings tumble over and over, thrashing their way toward the water, until lucky timing found them in the drawback of a wave that pulled them farther and farther out into the relative safety of the ocean, poking their little bean-sized heads above the water to gulp air. At least we pointed them in the right direction. A danger for young turtles is being unable to see the horizon because of human beach alteration or artificial lighting, or hear the pounding surf because of human noise interference. The hatchling then begins its pelagic life phase as passengers in the vast oceanic pool, bobbing in the ocean current for two to seven years, eating whatever the ocean's drift passes by.

At 100 pounds and 30 inches long, olive ridleys are the smallest sea turtle. They make up for their smaller size by their vast numbers. After joining in flotillas out in the open water, hundreds of olive ridley females come ashore over several nights for a mass egg laying event called an "arribada," Spanish for "arrival." The temperature of the sand determines the sex of the hatchlings. Warm sand between 82°-85° makes females, cool sand insures 100% males. Most hatchlings emerge under the cover of darkness for safety. Olive ridleys can dive to 950 feet looking for the invertebrates which make up their carnivorous diet of mollusks and crustaceans.

All seven populations of the world's sea turtles follow similar patterns, from egg to hatchling to pelagic existence through subadult to adult migrations. Between feeding, breeding, and nesting grounds, they travel some 1,200 miles or farther. Truly global citizens, sea turtles recognize no national boundaries or sovereign nations.

Mating takes place in the ocean, with the male using his "thumb" claw to grasp the female's carapace as he hangs on with his prehensile tail. The female must swim for both of them battling the wave action, rising to the surface to breathe every twenty minutes or so during their several-hour encounter.

When reaching the beach for nesting, females leave behind their elegance in the water and become ponderous and awkward on land. Trundling up onto the sandy beach beyond the high water line is exhausting for the moms without the watery support for their heavy bodies. They have to dig their two-foot-deep, seven-foot-wide nest, taking several hours before they can return to the safety of the sea. Females nest only every other year or take even longer between nesting cycles. They lay several clutches of eggs every season they do nest. Turtles can live up to 100 years, and it can take up to 30-50 years for a turtle to grow to maximum size and reach sexual maturity. Once they reach adulthood, only sharks or orcas can take them on. Many adult turtles bear the scars of encounters with these predators.

Each turtle becomes its own micro-desalinization plant, purging salt from its system via tear glands near the eyes. Their vision is strong in the water, but somewhat myopic above or out of water.

They use the same geomagnetic fields for navigating, migration, and orientation as do whales. Rare among animals, turtles are silent, but their sense of touch is highly acute. Because their shells provide an environment for microorganisms to hitch a ride, "cleaning fish" such as suckerfish, surgeonfish, and wrasses follow turtles like rock stars to eat the clinging organisms.

Sea turtles have been around for 100 million years. Some turtle ancestors, like the archelon from the Cretaceous era, were fifteen feet long with 16-foot flippers, weighing in at 4,850 pounds. Turtles, in general, pre-date dinosaurs.

Humans have long revered these reptiles as symbols of mystery, spirituality, wisdom and longevity. Turtles were found buried in Arabian graves from 6,000 years ago. Hawaiians drew turtle petroglyphs. Egyptians may have been the first to harvest them to make jewelry, harkening back to Queen Hatshepsut.

From Columbus's time, turtles have been overharvested. Sailors saw them as fresh meat, carting away the helpless females from nesting beaches and storing them upside down in the holds of ships, sometimes leaving them in that agony for months at a time. Being killed for their meat, eggs, oil, leather, and products made from their shells further decimated populations.

Turtles try to eat anything passing by, which can be deadly when it's human trash. Pollution, commercial driftnets and gillnets, military actions, oil production, boat strikes, and overbuilding on beaches are some of the reasons all sea turtles are now considered endangered. A horrific disease called fibropapillomatosis has attacked turtles worldwide, causing the growth of warty tumors. This turtle cancer has been found to have a direct correlation between pollution from shore and the turtles which have to swim in it.

Like the slow-moving creatures they are, sea turtles have a hard time adapting to change. So, it's up to us, the ones who caused many of their problems and altered their world, who find the solutions to make it habitable and safe for these ancient beings that go with the ocean's flow once again.

Conclusion

I fell in love with every single animal I encountered – OK – maybe not the scorpions. But as I dug deeper into the research on each creature, I realized the tenuous strands of life today are being stretched to the limits of, and sometimes beyond, the breaking point. We're approaching seven billion people on our planet, and we can feel it in the ever-increasing amount of traffic and crowds as we all want to do the same things at the same time in the same places.

What must the animals be feeling?

Encounters in the wild make my heart sing. Observing a herd of deer melt into the trees and then vanish, or glimpsing a hawk soar overhead, produces a lightness in my soul that remains long after the creature has disappeared.

We all feel better when our lives are in balance and harmony. Let things go out of whack, and we start feeling unsettled and stressed. Let things go on badly for an extended period of time, and it truly alters our minds and our lives. Think "rats in a cage" experiments.

There are two kinds of people in the world today – those who feel connected to the natural world, and those who feel separate from it. We must help those people to understand that animals possess both intelligence and emotions. We don't know exactly how many creatures share this fragile planet with us. Estimates range from between two to eight million distinctly different species here on Earth.

So, what can we do to nurture the connectedness to nature so vital to us all?

First of all, get out in nature as much as possible. Cultivate an aching love and reverence for wild lands. Bring the kids and the grandkids to forests and deserts, canyons and mountains, oceans and oases, so they can experience that awe and appreciate it. People don't protect anything unless they experience the wonder for themselves and fall in love with it.

Visit and support your national and state parks. For all their foibles and problems, they are still America's best idea, and a stalwart against unwise short-sighted development. Pay attention to local politics and protest any changes in land use that impinges on animal habitat. Belong to organizations that dedicate themselves to wise and forward-thinking land and animal preservation. Read about the world's amazing animals, and travel when you can to see their unique ecosystems, and/or watch *National Geographic*. And never lose your sense of wonder when you are lucky enough to encounter an animal on its turf, living out its natural life.

There is intrinsic value in untouched places and wild animals. Own your part in preserving and maintaining this mutual state for well-being. Seek out that oneness often. Go out there. Revel in it.

Acknowledgements

Thanks to librarians everywhere for being ready to enlighten, and especially the reference librarians at the Flagstaff Public Library. They got used to my coming in and nosing around; and they began asking, "So, what animal are you working on now?"

Special thanks go to Michael Quinn, Visual Information Specialist for Grand Canyon National Park, and Susan McGlothlin, formerly of Northern Arizona University's Cline Library, Special Collections. Both helped me track down photos of the Havasupai Ram Dancers, Guardians of the Canyon, so I could refresh my memory about that long-ago ceremony I witnessed.

A huge expression of thanks goes to the Northern Arizona Authors Association. This wonderful group of exceptional authors listened to me read chapters from this book month after month, offering constructive criticism, encouragement, fact checking and praise. Really, I couldn't have done it without your support.

For the Flagstaff Writers Group, listening to you week after week reminds me of what good writing is—and what I should aspire to.

Thanks again to artist and writer ValJesse O'Feeney for bringing all these animals to life with her wonderful illustrations.

There aren't enough superlatives to express my gratitude to my outstanding editor, Donna Reese. You stuck with me through this long project. Your many excellent suggestions made every chapter I sent you a stronger, better piece. Thank you.

To Allison Hays, for giving me permission to share her mountain lion story—without a doubt the most amazing encounter ever.

To Tom Martin & Hazel Clark at Vishnu Temple Press —thank you so much for your professionalism, expertise, unflappable spirit, and friendship. It is a pleasure working with you both.

And finally, to my wonderful husband, Keith, who believed in this book enough to share his animal encounters and take time from the writing of his Phantom Ranch book to help me finish this one. Thank you.

About the Illustrator

Valjesse O'Feeney, (aka Val Stannard) has been contributing artwork and photojournalism for over half a century. The published subjects she has been given awards for include horses, Western life, American frontier history, as well as a variety of wildlife. O'Feeney received formal training in southern California, Arizona and Banff School of Arts in Alberta, Canada.

When possible she likes to make live sketches, and has enjoyed that opportunity while raising orphaned or injured wildlife for the Fish and Game Departments of two countries. She has many treasured experiences of being followed into the woods by moose, deer, ravens and other creatures.

The artist can be reached at

P.O. Box 335, Williams, Arizona 86046

Bibliography

Alvin, Virginia. *The Peregrine Falcon.* Brookfield, Connecticut: Millbrook Press, 1995.

Anderson, Michael F. *Living at the Edge: Explorers, Exploiters and Settlers of the Grand Canyon Region.* Grand Canyon: Grand Canyon Association, 1998.

Areste, Manuel. *Snakes of the World.* Translated from Spanish by Gorg Blanc. New York: Sterling Publishing, Inc., 2003.

Arizona Game & Fish. "Elk." www.azgfd.gov. February 10, 2005.

Arnold, Caroline. *Australian Animals.* New York: Harper Collins Publishers, 2000.

Ayrey, Rich. www.azscorpion.com.

Barrett, Jalma. *Wildcats of North America: Bobcat.* Woodbridge, Connecticut: Blackbirch Press, Inc., 1999.

Bauer, Erwin A. *Mule Deer: Behavior, Ecology, Conservation.* Photographs by Erwin and Peggy Bauer. Stillwater, Minnesota: Voyageur Press, 1995.

Behrstock, Robert. *Dragonflies and Damselflies of the Southwest.* Tucson: Rio Nuevo Publishers, 2008.

Bennett, Jane, et al. *Watching Wildlife Australia.* Victoria, Australia: Lonely Planet Publications, Pty Ltd., 2000.

Breiter, Matthias. *Bears: A Year in the Life.* Buffalo, New York: Firefly Books, 2005.

British Antarctic Survey. *Antarctic Peninsula: A Visitor's Guide.* London: Natural History Museum, 2012.

Brown, Gary. *The Bear Almanac: A Comprehensive Guide to the Bears of the World.* Guilford, Connecticut: Lyons Press, 2009.

Byers, John A. *American Pronghorn: Social Adaptations and Ghosts of Predators Past.* Chicago: University of Chicago Press, 1997.

Cartaino, Carol. *Myths & Truths About Coyotes: What You Need to Know about America's Most Misunderstood Predator.* Birmingham, Alabama: Menasha Ridge Press, 2011.

Chadwick, Douglas. "Ghost Cats." *National Geographic Magazine,* December, 2013. 64-83.

Cleave, Andrew. *Snakes & Reptiles: A Portrait of the Animal World.* New York: Smithmark Publishers, Inc., 1994.

Cockrum, E. Lendell. *Mammals of the Southwestern United States & Northwestern Mexico: Selected Examples and Related Species.* Tucson: Treasure Chest Publications, Inc., 1992.

Darling, James D. *Whales, Dolphins and Porpoises.* Washington, D.C.: National Geographic Society, 1995.

Davis, Goode P. Jr. *Man and Wildlife in Arizona: The American Exploration Period, 1824-1865.* Published by the Arizona Game and Fish Department, in cooperation with the Arizona Cooperative Wildlife Research Unit, 1986.

Dennis, Ray. *Golden Eagles.* Grantown-on-Spey, Scotland: Colin Baxter Photography, Ltd., 1996.

Elliott, Lang. *The Frogs and Toads of North America: A Comprehensive Guide to their Identification, Behavior and Calls.* Harcourt, New York: Houghton Mifflin, 2009.

Ewing, Susan. *Shadow Cat: Encountering the American Mountain Lion.* Seattle: Sasquatch Books, 1999.

Geist, Valerius. *Antelope Country: Pronghorns: The Last Americans.* Photographs by Michael H. Francis. Iola, Wisconsin: Krause Publications, 2001.

Grolier Encyclopedia. *Elk.* USA: Scholastic Library Publishing, Inc., 2003. 241-42, 250.

Gulko, Dave & Eckert, Karen. *Sea Turtles: An Ecological Guide.* Honolulu: Mutual Publishing, 2004.

Heffelfinger, Jim. *Deer of the Southwest: A Complete Guide to the Natural History, Biology, and Management of Southwestern Mule Deer and White-Tailed Deer.* Texas: Texas A & M University Press, 2006.

————, James R. Purdue and Ken E. Nicolls. "Is Merriam's Elk Really Extinct?" *Arizona Wildlife Views Magazine,* January-February 2002, 6-10.

Henry, J. David. *Living on the Edge: Foxes.* Minocqua, Wisconsin: Northword Press, Inc., 1996.

————. *Red Fox: The Catlike Canine.* Washington, D.C.: Smithsonian Institution Press, 1986.

Hinshaw, Dorothy. *Eagles of America.* New York: Holiday House, 1995.

Houk, Rose. "Arizona's Elk." Flagstaff, Arizona: Earth Notes: *www.knau.org., October 3, 2012.*

Insight Guide: Peru. Long Island City, New York: Langenscheidt Publishers, Inc., 2008.

International Wildlife Encyclopedia. *Alpaca, Leopard Seal.* Terrytown, New York: Marshall Cavendish Corporation, 2002. 1449-50, 1470-72.

Jackson, Tom. *Animals of Asia & Australia.* London: Southwater Edition, 2004

Kavanagh, James. *The Nature of Arizona: An Introduction to Familiar Plants and Animals and Natural Attractions.* Blaine, Washington*: Waterford Press, 1996.*

Kobalenko, Jerry. *Forest Cats of North America: Cougars, Bobcats, Lynx.* Ontario, Canada: Firefly Books Ltd., 1997.

Lanting, Frans. *Penguins.* Koln, Germany: Benedikt Taschen Verlag Gmbh Hohenzollernring, 1999.

Looney, Dr. Robert N. "How Arizona was Restocked with Elk." *Arizona Wildlife Views Magazine,* January-February, 2003, 24-28.

Malotki, Ekkehart. *Hopi Coyote Tales :Istutuwutsi.* Lincoln, Nebraska: University of Nebraska Press, 1984.

Markle, Sandra. *Scorpions: Armored Stingers.* Minneapolis: Lerner Publications Company, 2011.

Mattison, Chris. *300 Frogs: A Visual Reference to Frogs and Toads from Around the World.* Buffalo, New York: Firefly Books, 2007.

————. *Frogs & Toads of the World*. New York: Facts on File Edition, 2002.

Meloy, Ellen. *Eating Stone: Imagination and the Loss of the Wild*. New York: Pantheon Books, 2005.

Nielsen, John. *Condor: To the Brink and Back – The Life and Times of One Giant Bird*. New York: Harper Collins Publishers, 2006.

Olin, George. *Mammals of the Southwest Deserts*. Globe, Arizona: Southwest Parks and Monuments Association, 1954.

Osborn, Sophie A. *Condors in Canyon Country: The Return of the California Condor to the Grand Canyon Region*. Grand Canyon: Grand Canyon Association, 2007.

O'Shea, Mark. *Reptiles and Amphibians*. New York: Dorling Kindersley Handbook, 1st American ed., 2001.

Parry-Jones, Jemima. *Eagles & Birds of Prey*. New York: Dorling Kindersley Publishing, Inc., 1997.

Perrine, Doug. *Sea Turtles of the World*. Stillwater, Minnesota: Voyageur Press, Inc., 2003.

Pringle, Laurence. *Scorpions! Strange and Wonderful*. Honesdale, Pennsylvania: Boyds Mills Press, Inc., 2013.

Ritchie, Tom. *The Antarctica Primer*. New York: Lindblad Expeditions, 2008.

Robinson, Gail. *Coyote the Trickster: Legends of the North American Indians*. New York: Crane, Russak & Company, Inc., 1976.

Russell, Charlie. *Grizzly Seasons: Life with the Brown Bears of Kamchatka*. Buffalo, New York: Firefly Books, 2003.

Russo, John P. *The Desert Bighorn Sheep in Arizona*. Phoenix: State of Arizona Game & Fish Department, 1956.

Sartore, Joel. *Face to Face with Grizzlies*. Washington, D.C.: National Geographic Society, 2006.

Savage, Candace. *Wild Cats: Lynx-Bobcats-Mountain Lions*. San Francisco: Sierra Club Books, 1993.

————. *Peregrine Falcons*. San Francisco: Sierra Club Books, 1992.

Shea, Rachel Hartigan. "Every Last One." Photographs by Joel Sartore. *National Geographic Magazine,* April, 2016. 74-85.

Sheldon, Charles. *The Wilderness of the Southwest.* Salt Lake City: University of Utah Press, 1993.

Simmonds, Mark. *Whales & Dolphins of the World.* Cambridge, Massachusetts: MIT Press, 2004.

Tekiela, Stan. *Mammals of Arizona: Field Guide.* Cambridge, Minnesota: Adventure Publications, Inc., 2008.

Tillett, Guy. *Ovis: North American Wild Sheep.* Photographs by Serle Chapman. Missoula, Montana: Mountain Press Publishing, 1997.

Weber, Steven A., ed. *Havasupai Habitat: A.F. Whiting's Ethnography of a Traditional Indian Culture.* Tucson: University of Arizona Press, 1985.

Whales, Dolphins and Porpoises. New York: Checkmark Books, An Imprint of Facts On File, Inc., 1999.

Wild, Paula. *The Cougar: Beautiful, Wild and Dangerous.* Madeira Park, British Colombia, Canada: McIntyre Ltd., 2013.

Williams, Zella. *Llamas and Other Latin American Camels.* First edition, bilingual version. New York: Rosen Publishing Group, 2010.

Witherington, Blair. *Sea Turtles: An Extraordinary Natural History of Some Uncommon Turtles.* St. Paul, Minnesota: Voyageur Press, 2006.

World Book Encyclopedia. *Deer.* Chicago: World Book, Inc., 1998. 61-3.

Yule, Lauray. *Coyotes.* Tucson: Rio Nuevo Publishers, 2004.

About the Author

Nancy Rivest Green was born in Massachusetts, then moved to Arizona with her family. There she finished high school, and attended the University of Arizona in Tucson. She embarked on a 28-year teaching career in the areas of Special Education, Elementary Education and School Librarian. Life changed forever for her after discovering the Grand Canyon, living and teaching in Grand Canyon National Park with her ranger husband. She won awards as a Special Education teacher and a School Librarian. Now retired and living on the edge of the Kaibab National Forest, she continues her love affair with nature and writing. She spends as much time hiking, kayaking, and bicycling as she can, except for when she's traveling or working on her new book. She can be reached at www.nancyrivestgreen.com.

Nancy's debut novel was *On the Brink of Shards,* a prehistoric adventure novel full of action which takes place in the Four Corners region. This novel won second place for the 2016 Arizona Authors Association's Novel of the Year.

Her next book is a children's alphabet book with a Southwestern flair and Spanish vocabulary words. It will encourage the young reader to search back through the book for all the alphabet pictures hidden throughout the story of this feisty little Hispanic girl.